Children and young people in custody

Managing the risk

Edited by Maggie Blyth, Robert Newman and Chris Wright

 Rainer crime concern

First published in Great Britain in 2009 by The Policy Press

The Policy Press
University of Bristol
Fourth Floor, Beacon House
Queen's Road
Bristol BS8 1QU
UK

Tel no +44 (0)117 331 4054
Fax no +44 (0)117 331 4093
E-mail tpp-info@bristol.ac.uk
www.policypress.org.uk

North American office:
The Policy Press
c/o International Specialized Books Services
920 NE 58th Avenue, Suite 300
Portland, OR 97213-3786, USA
Tel +1 503 287 3093
Fax +1 503 280 8832
e-mail info@isbs.com

© The Policy Press 2009

ISBN 978 1 84742 261 3

British Library Cataloguing in Publication Data
A catalogue record for this report is available from the British Library.

Library of Congress Cataloging-in-Publication Data
A catalog record for this report has been requested.

Cover image courtesy of www.johnbirdsall.co.uk
Cover design by Qube Design Associates, Bristol
Printed in Great Britain by Latimer Trend, Plymouth

Contents

Acknowledgements

We would like to thank everyone who contributed to this publication, including those who participated in a seminar in April 2008 that introduced many of the volume's themes. We are also grateful to the Youth Justice Board for England and Wales for providing financial support to the seminar and to Rainer Crime Concern for its help in organising the event. The views expressed in this volume are varied and do not necessarily reflect the views of the editors. We are grateful to all the contributors for adding to an important debate concerning children and young people in custody.

Foreword

I welcome this collection of essays on young people and the use of custody. For those, like me, who have spent most of their careers delivering services to children and young people in need, listening to them and their families, and also hearing the views and experiences of victims of crime (many of whom are children and young people themselves), there can be few more challenging subjects.

Over the past 10 years there has been a renewed focus on youth justice, with the establishment of the Youth Justice Board for England and Wales (YJB) in 1998 of which I was a founder member. Although, of late, it has been topical to be critical of the impact the YJB has had on the system, I simply refer the reader to the picture painted in the conclusion of this edition of the many improvements that have been delivered. It isn't perfect, and I am very aware of the serious consequences when things go wrong, but there have been some notable and worthy improvements, not only in the coordination of youth justice services and the involvement of an ever-widening range of agencies, but also in relation to the quality of care for those young people who do enter the secure establishments.

That said, there is clearly a great deal more that can be done. In my view, we need to focus seriously on reducing the numbers of youngsters entering the custodial system. As illustrated in this volume, too many young people are ending up in custody too quickly without having the benefit of alternative interventions, and many are subject to the vagaries of decision making by those responsible for sentencing. Despite the improvements in regime, there remains much more to be done in creating the 'therapeutic' conditions that are known to be effective in working with young people who, in the vast majority of cases, have been exposed to a multitude of disadvantages and where, in many instances, mainstream services have simply failed to respond or meet their needs.

This volume has made me think even harder about what I can contribute to the debate, including discussions about the need to raise the age of criminal responsibility and thus divert many children and young people from the criminal justice system into more appropriate services designed to focus specifically on their needs and behaviours.

Joyce Moseley OBE
Chief Executive, Rainer Crime Concern

Notes on contributors

Rob Allen is Director of the International Centre for Prison Studies at King's College London. He was previously Director of Rethinking Crime and Punishment at the Esmée Fairburn Foundation in London and, before that, Director of Research at the National Association for the Care and Resettlement of Offenders (Nacro) and Head of the Juvenile Offender Policy Unit in the Home Office. He was a member of the Youth Justice Board for England and Wales (YJB) for several years. He has extensive experience of international penal reform work, mainly in the field of young people.

Kerry Baker is a researcher at the Centre for Criminology, University of Oxford, and a consultant to the YJB on issues of assessment, risk and public protection. She has been closely involved in the development and validation of the ASSET assessment profile currently used by all Youth Offending Teams (YOTs) in England and Wales and has recently been responsible for developing guidance for youth justice staff on a range of public protection issues.

Maggie Blyth is currently the independent chair of Nottingham YOT management board and has been a member of the Parole Board for England and Wales since 2005. She was former Head of Practice at the YJB from 2001-05 and set up the Oxfordshire YOT in the 1990s. With a background in the probation service and youth justice, she continues to work extensively at international, national and local levels advising on youth justice policy and practice.

Deborah Coles has been the Co-director of INQUEST since 1990, the key non-government organisation that works directly with bereaved people following deaths in custody, which provides independent and legal advice on the investigation and inquest system. She is the chair of the national charity, Women in Prison, and a founding member and trustee of the Centre for Corporate Accountability, which works around the issue of workplace deaths. She is also the chair of the charity Buwan Koti International Trust.

Barry Goldson is Professor of Criminology and Social Policy at the University of Liverpool. He is the founding editor of *Youth Justice: An International Journal* (Sage) and his most recent books include: *In the care of the state? Child deaths in penal custody in England and Wales* (with Coles; INQUEST, 2005); *Youth crime and justice: Critical issues* (with Muncie; Sage, 2006); *Comparative youth justice: Critical issues* (with Muncie; Sage, 2006) and the *Dictionary of youth justice* (Willan, 2008). He is currently compiling and co-editing (with Muncie) a three-volume set of international 'major works' on youth crime and juvenile justice for the Sage Library of Criminology.

Hazel Kemshall is currently Professor of Community and Criminal Justice at De Montfort University. Her research interests include the assessment and management of high-risk offenders, multi-agency public protection panels and community responses to sexual offenders. She has written extensively on risk, public protection and dangerousness, and has completed research for the Home Office, the Scottish Executive and the Economic and Social Research Council.

Rod Morgan is Professor of Criminal Justice at the University of Bristol and Visiting Professor at the University of Cardiff and the London School of Economics and Political Science. He was previously HM Chief Inspector of Probation for England and Wales (2001-04) and Chairman of the Youth Justice Board (2004-07). He has written widely on policing and criminal justice issues and is co-editor of the *Oxford handbook of criminology* (2007 [4th edn], OUP) and the *Handbook of probation* (2007, Willan). He is also an adviser to the Council of Europe and Amnesty International on custodial conditions and the prevention of torture.

Robert Newman is Head of Inclusion at the YJB. He has held a range of policy roles at the Board, joining in 1999 with a remit to introduce a purchasing and commissioning system for the new juvenile secure estate before taking a lead on education policy. With a background in education and special needs, he has been responsible for several key policy initiatives for young people in the youth justice system and has also been an adviser to the Council of Europe, working recently in Macedonia.

Jim Rose is Director of the national charity, the Nurture Group Network. He has worked for many years in various types of secure accommodation for young people and published on the subject, most notably *From chaos to culture* (2002). From 1998 to 2001 he was professional adviser to the Home Office with responsibility for the placement and management of young people sentenced to long-term custody.

Chris Wright is the National Director, Operations and New Business, at Rainer Crime Concern. He was previously Head of Performance at the YJB from 2001 to 2006, where he was responsible for the youth justice performance framework across England and Wales and the secure estate for children and young people. Chris has worked extensively within the criminal justice system, establishing the Nottingham YOT in the 1990s after a career in the probation service.

Introduction

Maggie Blyth, Robert Newman and Chris Wright

Youth custody: the history

The number of children in custody in England and Wales has risen in recent years and is now the highest in Western Europe (Council of Europe, 2004). In July 2008, when this volume was completed, the numbers of young people held in the secure estate stood at 3,006 (YJB, 2008a). Overall, the rise in imprisonment is due to courts adopting a more punitive approach, locking up proportionately more children and for longer (Solomon and Garside, 2008). Both the public and media have driven the political agenda, reinforcing messages that youth crime, in particular, knife and gun crime, is out of control and should be dealt with by harsher sentences. And, despite recent sentencing guidelines, the new Lord Chief Justice has spoken of an 'epidemic' of knife crime requiring the 'most severe sentences'. These comments, like previous remarks linked to street robbery in 2001, are likely to lead to even tougher sanctions and use of custody for young people (*The Guardian*, 8 July 2008).

Although there have been attempts by the Youth Justice Board (YJB) to regulate the increase in youth custody by introducing alternative community packages such as the Intensive Supervision and Surveillance Programme (ISSP), this has not led to the reduction in custody anticipated by earlier commentators (Audit Commission, 2004). Nowhere have the figures been more stark than in the rapid rise of indeterminate sentences imposed on those young people under 18 years of age between 2006 and 2007, where numbers doubled during the year (YJB, 2008b). And, in terms of reducing further offending, prison has very little impact at all, with reoffending rates for young people leaving custody at 67% (YJB, 2008b). Furthermore, it is well documented that those young people returning to the community invariably face problems in accessing mainstream services and are often unable to sustain intentions to lead law-abiding lives (Audit Commission, 2004; HM Government, 2008b). These facts require probing if we really want to deal with the issue of youth offending across England and Wales. We fully accept that sanctions, including the proportionate use of custody, are necessary to curb violent and high-risk behaviour by young people, but we ask the question whether the rapid rise in the use of custodial sanctions is the most effective way of reducing youth crime. Can society afford to continue to deal with the punishment of young people in isolation from the problems that may draw them into offending in the first place?

Youth Crime Action Plan: the future

A decade into the youth justice reforms, there is a renewed focus on the priorities for tackling youth offending as set out in the Youth Crime Action Plan (YCAP) published in July 2008 (HM Government, 2008). Aside from the independent reviews of youth justice (Audit Commission, 2004; Solomon and Garside, 2008), YCAP is the first 'comprehensive cross government analysis' of youth justice services for a decade (HM Government, 2008, p 1). The document sets out a 'triple track approach' of 'enforcement and punishment where behaviour is unacceptable, non-negotiable support and challenge where it is most needed, and better and earlier prevention' (HM Government, 2008, p 1). It is a timely report and one that represents a shift in emphasis, with children's services having a more central role in the leadership and direction of youth justice services, although clearly still within the context of an enforcement philosophy. This shift is mirrored by the now joint ownership of the youth justice agenda by two government ministries. Whether this represents a sea change in government policy in relation to youth crime is unclear, as there remain inherent tensions in managing enforcement on the one hand and support measures on the other. Ministers are also clear that robust messages are required in response to the spate of stabbings seen mainly in the capital during 2007 and 2008. Gordon Brown himself has said: 'What I want to see is anybody using a knife goes to prison. Anyone who is carrying a knife is subject either to prison or strong community payback, so in all cases there is a presumption to prosecute' (*The Guardian*, 15 July 2008). The government's multifaceted approach to dealing with the causes of crime at an early stage, working with families and emphasising early intervention alongside enforcement, challenge and sanctions for non-compliance, is a recognition that there are no quick fixes to solving the problem of youth crime. The evidence base for early intervention is still developing, but there are emerging messages from the evaluation of key government prevention programmes that are important in assisting both practitioners and policy makers (Blyth and Solomon, 2008).

Moreover, although fresh consideration is given to the importance of resettlement work with young people leaving custody, the YCAP disappointingly steers clear of any radical overhaul of the current secure estate for children and young people. In prioritising prevention work there is an expectation that resources should be directed towards early intervention, but it is debatable whether even the announcements of serious investment by government in this area will significantly buck the current custodial trend, particularly in dealing with problems associated with violence. However, the opportunity for more engagement with wider children's services in relation to those most troubled youngsters at risk of offending is certainly possible, with new duties placed on children's services in relation to the planning and commissioning of offender education and with the debate now in full swing about who should be held responsible for the real costs associated with incarceration. Directors of children's services will be required to engage closely with Youth Offending Teams (YOTs) and the wider youth justice system, holding other key partners to account to ensure that key outcomes related to youth offending are delivered, in particular those related to targeted early intervention, educational attainment and resettlement activity.

Prior to the publication of the YCAP, there have been other calls for a review of youth custody during 2008. The Prison Reform Trust published a briefing note setting out 12 ways of reducing the numbers of children in custody (Prison Reform Trust, 2008). Interestingly, among the measures was a recommendation for transferring custodial budgets to local authorities as well as suggestions for a range of measures to ensure that children's services (with YOTs) prioritise other packages such as intensive fostering, bail supervision and improving services to looked after children and those with mental health needs. In addition, all children's commissioners in the UK reported in June 2008 that 'too many children are being criminalised and brought into the youth justice system at an increasingly young age' (UK Children's Commissioners, 2008: para 171, 32).

This volume brings together contributions from experts to critically examine government policy in relation to the incarceration of children and young people under the age of 18. It remarks on the policy and direction of the government in the context of the 'three track approach' outlined in the YCAP, and reviews the aspirations of the YJB over the last decade in relation to its strategy for the children's secure estate. Consideration is given to the sort of regime considered most effective for young people, whether there is scope, or indeed political will, in moving away from large establishments dominated by the Prison Service to smaller units based in local communities. And questions are asked about whether the outcomes that impact on youth offending may be more effectively driven by children's services, particularly in relation to educational attainment. The collection of contributions in this volume consider the purpose of secure establishments and query who should be held responsible for bearing the cost of custody and the resettlement of children and young people back into the community. Moreover, at a time of public and political pressure reinforcing a punitive model for youth crime, the contributions draw out the safeguarding implications of the current custodial estate in relation to children and young people. How should practitioners balance the multiple needs of young people in the youth justice system against a prevailing preoccupation with public protection and risk management? This issue remains a finely balanced one (Blyth et al, 2007).

Three themes remain integral to the volume and are given scrutiny: the suitability of current custodial regimes to deal with the multiple problems facing many young people sentenced to custody and the safeguarding implications arising from this; the scope for more effective resettlement opportunities with closer links to mainstream services; and the need to review who should be accountable for the commissioning and placement of secure beds. These themes are examined with regard to current sentencing practice and decisions about the release of young people from custody.

1. The secure estate for children and young people: is it fit for purpose?

The YJB outlined its plans and aspirations for youth custody in its Strategy for the Secure Estate for Children and Young People (YJB, 2005a) and, in recognition of the Children Act 2004 and the Every Child Matters agenda, the focus was centred on the need for a child and young person centred culture, with staff committed to working with children and young people who were adequately trained in this area of work. Efforts were made to encourage Prison Service staff to complete nationally approved training in effective work with juveniles and significant resources were made available to ensure that regimes were geared to the needs of children and not disrupted by unnecessary transfers. The behaviour management approach developed by the YJB in 2006 emphasised positive encouragement and reward of young people. Yet the controversial use of physical restraint in the secure estate has continued, with a Court of Appeal only quashing the secure training centre amended rules, which allowed the use of restraint for 'good order and discipline', in August 2008. As the contributions in this volume suggest, there remain entrenched problems in the management of children and young people in custody.

Rod Morgan (Chapter 1) revisits the strategy and the general policy thrust of custody provision under the YJB since its inception in 1998, charting the progress of the reforms over the decade before the publication of the YCAP in July 2008. Jim Rose (Chapter 2) provides a historical analysis of the different regimes for children and young people in England and Wales, stating that the constituent elements of any secure regime must include relevant education, appropriate healthcare, mental health provision, offending behaviour work, links to families and resettlement opportunities, delivered in settled units without the continuing churn of moving numbers. In their chapter on deaths in custody (Chapter 5), Barry Goldson and Deborah Coles call for an independent inquiry into the use of youth custody and demand that lessons are learned from the deaths of children in custody over the last few years.

It seems likely that there remains a need to incarcerate a small number of young people who remain a continuing high risk to local communities and whose behaviour is unacceptable to the public. The government estimates that this accounts for 5% of young people in the youth justice system (HM Government, 2008). The question that remains outstanding is what is the most effective regime for these young people, given that a significant number reoffend on release and remain detached from mainstream services.

2. Resettlement

The government has announced extra funding to extend the current resettlement and aftercare programmes (RAP) across England and Wales and devotes a section of the YCAP to the rehabilitation of young people leaving prison, with particular regard to improving resettlement opportunities. This new emphasis on resettlement is to be welcomed but there have been warm words before, notably in the National Youth Resettlement Framework (YJB, 2005b), and translating the rhetoric into practical application on the ground will be the true test. There is evidence that by providing a package of resettlement support to 15 to 17 year olds the savings to the Treasury would be in the region of over £80 million a year (Rainer/RESET, 2007). Reinvesting such savings in targeted prevention programmes could go a long way to reducing the numbers of youngsters ending up in custody.

The YJB itself has remained committed to looking at smaller, higher intensity units for accommodating certain children and young people and attempting to locate young people as close to home and community as possible. One such unit will open at HMP Wetherby in October 2008. In their chapter considering a possible hybrid order to sit alongside the Detention and Training Order (DTO), Maggie Blyth and Robert Newman (Chapter 6) explore the merits of a new residential placement underpinned by education and linked to the forthcoming legislative duties placed upon local authorities to plan and commission education provision for young people in custody.

3. Making the costs of custody visible

The YCAP pulls together a number of proposals that when taken together represent a significant step towards local authorities becoming accountable for what happens in custody. New duties in relation to education have already been mentioned. The precedence for greater accountability in relation to funding secure beds is already set with secure remands into local authority care, where local authorities are required to fund one third of placement costs on the basis that they retain statutory responsibility for the young person in a way that they do not under sentencing legislation. The YCAP proposes making local authorities responsible for the whole cost. Rob Allen (Chapter 3) argues that the huge funds spent on incarcerating young people could be better used investing in prevention and early intervention schemes, and he puts forward ideas for properly considering the cost of custody. It is notable that the YJB used 64% of its total funding to purchase secure accommodation in 2006-07 (Solomon and Garside, 2008). This covered the purchase of beds in secure units across young offender institutions (YOIs), secure training centres (STCs) and secure children's homes (SCHs). Only a relatively small amount of money was spent in a similar period by the YJB on prevention projects.

Furthermore, there is a strong case for more effective links between local authorities and the courts. Although most YOTs will have established youth court user groups and strong strategic liaison with sentencers, there is inevitably little coordination between children's services and the courts. Kerry Baker (Chapter 4) demonstrates the importance of maintaining a distinction between the sentencing of young people and adults in her analysis of the complexity of sentencing decisions.

Hazel Kemshall (Chapter 7) explores how parole decisions in relation to young people are being affected by increasing public concern over high-risk cases, and points out that the use of a predominantly adult focus towards determining release may not be the right approach in dealing with adolescents. This has implications for the cost of custody in terms of safeguarding children's rights and child-centred practice. Following key judicial reviews, the Parole Board has reviewed some of its policy and practice in relation to juveniles and has issued new guidance about parole and young people. However, if young people are being detained in custody for longer periods because of problems in assessing reductions in risk or difficulties in assembling resettlement plans, this is concerning. It becomes vital to ensure that local children's services have greater involvement with young people sentenced to custody, with oversight for reviewing particular cases before release.

Summary

In conclusion, the publication of the YCAP in the summer of 2008 has arguably turned the focus of youth crime onto prevention and early intervention alongside enforcement. There are persuasive arguments that place youth justice services under the umbrella of children's trusts at local level with oversight from the Department for Children, Schools and Families (DCSF). What is less clear is whether new investment in early intervention will lead to any meaningful reduction in the custodial population. The contributions in this volume are diverse in their enquiry, but all seek to review the current secure estate for children and young people and the sentencing decisions that are leading to the greater use of incarceration. While some experts are bleaker in their analysis of the current direction of government policy with regard to youth custody, we hope that, in presenting a range of views, we can demonstrate the opportunity for policy change to address some of the systemic failings outlined.

References

Audit Commission (2004) *Youth justice 2004: A review of the reformed youth justice system*, London: Audit Commission.

Blyth, M. and Solomon, E. (2008) *Prevention and youth crime: Is early intervention working?*, Bristol: The Policy Press.

Blyth, M., Solomon, E. and Baker, K. (2007) *Young people and risk*, Bristol: The Policy Press.

Council of Europe (2004) *Space I, Council of Europe annual penal statistics*, Survey 2004, Strasbourg: Council of Europe.

HM Government (2008) *Youth Crime Action Plan*, London: COI.

Prison Reform Trust (2008) *Briefing paper*, London: Prison Reform Trust.

Rainer/RESET (2007) *The business case for youth resettlement*, London: RESET.

Solomon, E. and Garside, R. (2008) *Ten years of Labour's youth justice reforms: An independent audit*, London: Centre for Crime and Justice Studies.

YJB (Youth Justice Board) (2005a) *Strategy for the secure estate for children and young people*, London: YJB.

YJB (2005b) *Youth resettlement: A framework for action*, London: YJB.

YJB (2008a) Internal management information (unpublished).

YJB (2008b) *Youth Justice annual workload data 2006/7*, London: YJB.

UK Children's Commissioners (2008) Report to UN Committee on the Rights of the Child, London: 11 Million.

Children in custody

Rod Morgan

Introduction

In 2000 the Youth Justice Board (YJB), created by the Crime and Disorder Act 1998, sought and was given responsibility for commissioning and purchasing all custodial places in England and Wales required for children and youths by the criminal courts by virtue of their remand and sentencing decisions. The Board took on provision for what is proportionately the largest population of children in penal custody in Western Europe. It was arguably a poisoned chalice. This chapter will consider three questions. What, over the past decade, has been the trend regarding use of custody for children and youths and who are the young people in custody? How is the provision of custody for children organised, managed and made accountable? And what are the prospects for change?

Population trends and characteristics

It is a commonplace that any aspect of social policy considered over so short a period as 10 years is likely to make little sense without an understanding of the broader historical and political context. This is certainly the case when it comes to the peculiarly British addiction to punishment of the young and resort to their custody (see Morgan, 2007, pp 201-8; Morgan and Newburn, 2007, Chapter 30). For present purposes it must suffice to say that when New Labour came to power in 1997 they inherited a surge in the numbers of children in custody but introduced policies that did nothing effectively to reverse that upward trend. Indeed, in several important respects, Labour took further their Conservative predecessors' punitive approach, all part of their electoral winning mantra of being 'tough on crime, tough on the causes of crime', priority being given to the first part of that equation. Nor, during their subsequent victorious electoral campaigns, did Labour demonstrate any embarrassment about the record high numbers of young offenders in custody. They never maintained that the number of *children* in custody was an achievement, but, in 2001, 'arresting, convicting, punishing and rehabilitating persistent young offenders' was a key policy undertaking (Labour Party, 2001, p 32), and in 2005 the fact that they had built 'over 16,000 more prison places [additional places, which included those for young offenders] than there were in 1997' was reported as an achievement (Labour Party, 2005, p 3). There were to be, as Labour's key policy statement on youth justice proclaimed in 1997, *No more excuses* (Home Office, 1997).

A new sentence, the Secure Training Order (STO) of between six months and two years for 12 to 14 year olds, to be served in a new type of establishment, a secure training centre (STC), had been introduced by the Conservatives in 1994. It was to sit below the principal custodial provision for 15 to 17 year olds, detention of between two months and two years in a young offender institution (YOI). The STO was controversial because it lowered from 15 the age at which sentencers could normally consider custody and, second, the sentence was to be served in establishments built for the purpose, the management of which was to be contracted out to commercial providers. Labour retained this extension and relaxed the criteria restricting its use. They combined both sentences by introducing the Detention Training Order (DTO) for 12 to 17 year olds, a sentence of between four months' and two years' duration, of which the first half is spent in custody. They also replaced the strict criteria for offenders under 15 relating to 'persistence' with the provision that the sentence was available where the court 'is of the opinion that he is a persistent offender'. The courts interpreted this power rather broadly (see Ball et al, 2001, Chapter 28). These shorter sentences, available to the magistrates' courts, sit alongside continued provisions whereby serious offences – in the case of murder, mandatorily – are committed to the Crown Court and are liable to 'long-term detention' (to distinguish the sentence from a DTO) for which the maximum period for a child or young person is the same as that for an adult. These long-term detention cases are known as section 90 or 91 cases (2000 Powers of the Criminal Courts [Sentencing] Act).

The rise in the number of children and young people in custody under New Labour has slackened compared with that during the last years of the Conservative administration. In 1991, for example, there was less than half the number today. Further, although the population trend remains upwards, the average daily population at the time of writing (summer 2008) remains below the peak population in 2002 (at the time of the government's street crime initiative regarding robbery) and, very importantly, the *proportionate* use of custody has fallen in recent years (Ministry of Justice, 2007, Tables 1.5). The reason why the custodial population continues to grow, albeit at a slower rate than for adults, is that the overall number of children and young people criminalised has increased substantially – by 28% in the period 2002-07 (YJB, 2008) – and the average sentence length has increased for those sentenced to custody. If indeterminate sentences are excluded, the average sentence length for boys increased from 9.2 months in 1998 to 10.6 in 2006; that for girls increased from 7.1 to 8.3 months (Ministry of Justice, 2007, Table 2.5).

What explains this more punitive trend? There is no analysis of this question for children similar to that available for adults (see Hough et al, 2003) for whom, overwhelmingly, the evidence indicates that like-for-like offences are being dealt with more severely today than was formerly the case. Some change in offence mix is part of the answer – robbery and offences against the person now account for a significantly greater proportion of receptions as well as the average daily population of young offenders in custody than was previously the case. But it is difficult to draw conclusions from the data given the wide range of behaviours and levels of seriousness that these offence categories encompass (robbery, for example, includes forms of bullying such as 'taxing' fellow school pupils for their pocket money and taking an old lady's handbag at knifepoint). What has not changed significantly over the past decade is the criminal history of young offenders being dealt with by the courts (Home Office, 2007, para 6.13 and Table 6.5), though the proportion of offenders with many pre-convictions in custody has. Eighteen per cent were recorded as having no previous convictions in 1993 compared with 17% in 2001, whereas 20% had seven or more compared with 21% in 2001 (Home Office, 2003, Table 3.6). Contrary to what is widely believed, a significant proportion of young offenders committed to custody are not prolific offenders: well over one third, 37%, have no or only one or two previous offences, albeit those offences may be and often are serious.

The consequence of these trends is that the average number of children and young people in custody has increased by 13% in the period 1997-2007 (see Table 1.1).

Table 1.1: Children and young people in penal custody

	1997	1999	2001	2003	2005	2007
Secure children's homes	95	90	258	292	238	226
Secure training centres	–	55	118	185	248	257
Young offender institutions	2,479	2,422	2,415	2,267	2,339	2,431
Total	2,574	2,567	2,791	2,744	2,825	2,914

Source: Youth Justice Board, personal communication

Who are these children and young people in custody? They are overwhelmingly 16 and 17 year olds (78%, see Figure 1.1) and male (93%), though in recent years the increase in the number of girls has been greater than for boys, albeit during any one year the female population fluctuates much more than it does for boys (in 2006-07 it ranged from 180 to 242 – see YJB, 2008: 41). This volatility makes for operational difficulties beyond those resulting from seasonal variation (in 2006-07 the overall population ranged from approaching 3,100 in August to below 2,800 in December).

In 2006-07, 22% of this population were on remand and, of those who were sentenced, the overwhelming majority, 78%, were serving DTO sentences, although a disturbing minority of those serving more than two years, 116 out of 510, were subject to indeterminate sentences, including those for public protection (IPP sentences introduced by the Criminal Justice Act 2003, s 226 and s 228). This parallels the greater than anticipated use of such sentences for adults (for a general critique, see Prison Reform Trust, 2007).

Of the sentenced population, robbery (31%), violence against the person (26%), burglary (16%), vehicle theft or unauthorised taking (6%) are the most common principal offences. This pattern represents a change. A decade ago the proportion

Figure 1.1: Average custodial population age profile, 2006-07

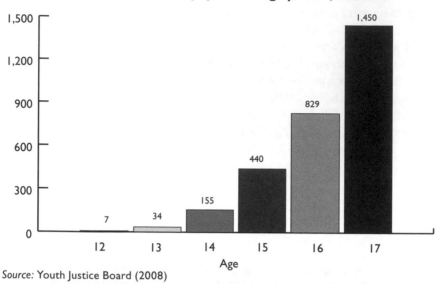

Source: Youth Justice Board (2008)

of young offenders in custody for violence and robbery offences was significantly lower than today and the contribution of burglary was far greater (Home Office, 2003, Table 3.11). Moreover, a growing proportion, currently 18%, of young people have been imprisoned for breach of community orders, reflecting the increasingly numerous prohibitions or demands built into community orders and the tighter enforcement of those orders (YJB, 2008, p 38).

Most of the young people committed to custody are there for a remarkably short time. In 2006-07, if remands are included, the average stay was 76 days. The average stay for DTO prisoners was 114 days or three and a half months. This is very little time to get to know the young people, let alone address the typically multiple problems they have.

A good deal is known from standard recording and epidemiological surveys about the characteristics of the children and young people in custody. A very high proportion, 27% in 2006-07, are non-white, black and mixed race being the largest minority groups (YJB, 2008, p 38).

The survey evidence indicates that the young people are drawn from the most deprived and socioeconomically marginalised sections of the community, and typically exhibit multiple problems. Regarding mental health, for example, 31% have identifiable problems. Almost one fifth suffer from depression, a tenth having engaged in an act of self-harm in the preceding month, similar proportions suffering from anxiety and post-traumatic stress disorder symptoms (PTSD), 7% suffering from hyperactivity and 5% suffering from psychotic-like symptoms. Almost one quarter have learning difficulties (that is, a measured IQ of less than 70) with a further third exhibiting borderline learning difficulties (a measured IQ of 70-80) (Harrington and Bailey, 2005).

These data are difficult to interpret. Do they reflect intrinsic learning difficulties, or an absence of intellectual stimulation, or both? A recent survey of young offenders receiving DTOs indicates that two thirds have been excluded from education, that four in 10 have at some stage in their lives been in the care of a local authority and that 17% have been placed on a child protection register (Hazel et al, 2002; see also HMIP, 2005). The result is that children in custody typically have a literacy and numeracy age some four to five years below their chronological age.

Their problems are contributed to or exacerbated by substance abuse. A recent study found that: 40% have been dependent on a substance at some point in their lives; 74% report having drunk alcohol more than once a week, with the majority of the drinkers regularly exceeding six units of alcohol on a single drinking occasion; 83% are smokers; 30% report that they have taken drugs not to get high but just to 'feel normal'; 38% say they have taken a drug to 'forget everything' or 'blot everything out' (Galahad SMS Ltd, 2004). The latter represents drug taking as a form of self-medication.

For all these reasons the YJB, on taking responsibility for commissioning custodial places for children in 2000, invested heavily in improving both the facilities and the programmes they inherited, so that the chronic needs of young offenders are better met, particularly in establishments run by the Prison Service. In 1997 the Chief Inspector of Prisons, in a coruscating thematic report, found that Prison Service provision for young offenders was 'chaotic' and did 'not constitute a system at all'; that there was an absence of vision, leadership and responsibility for this category of offender; that they were essentially 'warehoused' in institutions that were too big and in which bullying was 'endemic', there being little or no organisational recognition of their child status and considerable needs (HMIP, 1997, pp 69-70). In recent years, the Inspectorate has found the system generally improved, though still wanting in many respects, and a distinct risk, given current overcrowding, of early gains being lost (HMIP, 2003, p 34; 2004, p 44; 2005, pp 56-60; 2007, p 40; 2008, p 49).

Governance, organisation and accountability

Custodial provision for children in England and Wales is based on what is termed, in Whitehall jargon, a 'purchaser-provider' split, an arrangement designed to foster competition and maximise value for money. Since April 2000 the YJB has been responsible for commissioning and purchasing the custodial places that the courts, through their individual remand and sentencing decisions, implicitly demand. The Board currently purchases 3,420 beds (YJB, 2008, p 39) in three categories of establishments managed by central state, local state and commercial providers:

- 2,899 beds in YOIs, all but two of which are managed by the Prison Service. Commercial companies manage beds in two further institutions. YOI provision is for 15 to 17 year olds in the case of boys and 17 year olds in the case of girls. There are currently 13 institutions or units within institutions for males and four units for girls. Of these institutions all but five are split-site establishments. That is, the young offenders are held in more or less discrete sections of institutions, which also house prisoners aged 18 or over. The degree to which there is contact between the young and adult offenders varies according to the nature, layout and facilities in each establishment, though the YJB's aim (YJB, 2005) is to move gradually towards greater separation. Since separation will best be achieved in institutions exclusively for young offenders, we can expect, unless the custodial population rises and makes the strategy impossible, the YJB gradually to withdraw from most split-site arrangements. Until 2005 these split sites were shared with young adults (aged 18 to 20) but henceforth, as a result of legislative changes, the adult sections may accommodate prisoners aged 21 or over.
- 286 beds in four STCs, all of which are managed by commercial companies. The STCs, which are relatively small compared with most YOIs, are subdivided into small living units of six to eight beds. They generally accommodate adolescents in the middle age range of 14 to 16 years, though they also accommodate some older young people considered too vulnerable to be housed in the YOIs and, on occasion, younger children for whom there are no spaces available in secure children's homes (SCHs).
- 226 beds in 15 SCHs, all of which were until recently managed by local authorities (thus generally known as LASCHs) but one of which was in 2005 sold to a commercial operator. The SCHs vary in size, but are mostly very small and, like the STCs, are subdivided into small living units of six to eight beds. Children under the age of 15 are invariably housed in the SCHs but these homes also accommodate the occasional older adolescent considered too vulnerable to place in a YOI or an STC.

Placement of all children and young people remanded or sentenced to custody is initially undertaken by the YJB, which operates something akin to a call centre, which is notified by the local Youth Offending Teams (YOTs) of court decisions and the age and characteristics of the young people concerned. This is the YJB's only operational function and, it should be noted, the YJB is dependent on the quality of the risk assessments undertaken by the YOTs.

The average number of children and young people held in the 3,420 beds currently purchased by the YJB (see Table 1.1) may appear to suggest that typically the Board has approaching 15% spare capacity and operational room for manoeuvre. This is not the case. Quite apart from seasonal population fluctuations, the YOIs normally accommodate several hundred 18 or even 19 year olds. In summer 2005, for example, just over 500 (or 16%) of the 3,169 children and young people held in YJB-commissioned accommodation were aged 18 or over (Morgan, 2007, pp 212-13). They were young offenders who had attained the age of 18 during the course of their sentence and who the YJB placements team and the YOI (rarely, an 18 year old may also be found in an STC or SCH) had agreed should not be transferred to an adult establishment prior to the custodial part of their sentence expiring. Such agreements are made for offenders serving DTOs on the grounds that transferring them to adult establishments would be inhumane and counter-productive in terms of continuity in offender or educational programme participation. (Long-term offenders, depending on how long they have left to serve, are normally transferred on or shortly after attaining the age of 18.)

The consequence of this positive arrangement is that YJB-commissioned accommodation is typically close to full, with the YJB having precious little room for placements and operational manoeuvre and many more young people being held distant from their community roots than everyone, including the YJB, considers desirable. In 2005-06 approximately one third of all boys and half of all girls were being held in institutions more than 50 miles from home (YJB, 2007a, p 36), an aspect of system overcrowding about which the Prisons Inspectorate was increasingly critical (HMIP, 2007, p 43).

The Prisons Inspectorate also takes the view that most YOIs and living units within YOIs are too large. This, however, is the estate that the YJB has inherited and it will not easily be changed without either a substantial reduction in the custodial population or a significant increase in the YJB's budget, the prospects for both of which seem unlikely. Seventy per cent of the YJB's budget is already spent on purchasing custodial places and its budget is severely constrained. Further, although the Board has a target of reducing the number of children in custody, it is failing in that objective (which the YJB can only influence as opposed to determine) and publicly admits that it is unlikely to meet it (YJB, 2007b, p 26; see also Solomon and Garside, 2008, pp 47-8). If YOIs were to be less intensively used and the size of YOI living units reduced then custodial unit costs would inevitably rise. It already costs on average £53,112 per annum to keep a young offender in a YOI, £172,260 in an STC and £185,532 in an SCH (East Potential, 2008, pp 66-7). These substantial differences are largely accounted for by the very different staffing ratios.

All establishments for young offenders are regularly independently inspected: the YOIs by the Prisons Inspectorate and the STCs and SCHs by the Commission for Social Care Inspectorate (CSCI). In addition, each YOI has an independent monitoring board of lay persons attached to them and the YJB provides child advocates and social workers in every institution to assist the young inmates to find their voice and safeguard them from a child protection standpoint. The YJB also employs field staff to monitor compliance with the legal contracts it has with the STCs and SCHs and the service level agreement it has with the Prison Service. These contracts and agreements have been backed by significant investment to raise the standards of education, health and other provision required (see YJB, 2003, pp 30-5; YJB, 2004, pp 24-7). Successive inspectorate reports, though agreeing with the YJB's assessment that 'there is still a long way to go' (YJB, 2005, para 2), testify to the progress that has been made (see HMIP reports cited above).

The purchaser-provider split may be intended to achieve market competition and maximise the standards achieved and efficiencies gained, but in practice the YJB has little commissioning room for manoeuvre. Though the SCHs are geared to the intensive care of children, local authorities are not queueing up to open secure accommodation units and those already providing them will do so only if they can more or less guarantee that their beds will be filled and that the high costs will be more than covered. The evidence from recent years suggests that, were the YJB to terminate any of the existing SCH contracts, the units would be likely to close (four SCHs closed during the period 2001-05 for precisely this reason). At the other end of the spectrum, the Prison Service currently accommodates a total population of approximately 84,000 prisoners. The 4 to 5% of that population comprising young offenders is a relatively marginal consideration within that broader framework and, as successive Chief Inspectors of Prisons have emphasised, the management of young offenders within the Prison Service is arguably not given the distinct priority that critics consider necessary. Despite the appointment of a Director for Juveniles and Women, the Prison Service lines of management accountability are principally from governors to regional managers. Furthermore, prison governors operate within a web of standards and internal audits that are overwhelmingly geared to the adult prison population.

Between these two historical providers are the three commercial companies providing the four STCs, controversially established prior to the establishment of the YJB. The other providers regard the STCs with suspicion, particularly the SCHs, whose costs they most closely approximate and whose provision they have to some extent displaced. The principled and empirical proposition that the provision of secure custody for children is unsuitable for profitable enterprise and the argument that, wherever that market is allowed to develop, corners will be cut and lower standards are likely to prevail, continues to be widely subscribed to by social work practitioners and some penal pressure groups (for a statement opposing the contracting out of custodial provision for children, see Howard League, 2005).

It follows that all the current forms of custodial provision for children and young offenders involve operational shortcomings and dilemmas. The Prison Service is an organisational tanker, difficult to turn round, the staff insufficiently child-centred, despite the minimal training for working with children that the YJB is funding, and provides premises, many of which are unsuitable. STC staff, most of whom have no prior experience or qualifications for working with children, let alone the most difficult in the land, arguably have insufficient training to develop the skills they need. There is at present no central, strategic management or funding of the SCHs by central government and thus the aggregate supply of places is uncertain. The local authorities may not seek profits in the Marxist sense as, in the eyes of some, the commercial companies that run the STCs do, but they do not aim to make a loss either and their costs vary.

Many of these difficulties are reflected in the tragic deaths that have in recent years blighted the youth custody system. Fifteen children and young people have died in custody since 1997 (see Coles and Goldson, 2005), 14 by suicide and one while being restrained, two of these deaths in STCs and 13 in YOIs. Some of these cases have attracted considerable media attention. In some cases this has been due to what has been perceived to be scandalously inappropriate sentencing and placement decisions, a key example being the death of Joseph Scholes, aged 16, at Stoke Heath YOI in 2002, a case in which the inquest coroner called for a public inquiry subsequently denied by the government. In other cases, attention has focused on what has been held to be the inappropriate behaviour of staff, as in the case of Gareth Myatt, aged 15 and weighing seven stone, who died while being restrained by three members of staff at Rainsbrook STC in 2004. No member of staff was prosecuted in the latter case but a subsequent Howard League inquiry report (Carlile, 2006) was scathing about the culture of physical restraint existing in the STCs and the shortcomings of the youth custody system generally.

What justifies the very different costs incurred for the three sections of the custodial estate and which, if escort costs are included, account for such a high proportion of the YJB's budget? There is no straightforward answer to this question. The YOIs, STCs and SCHs cannot easily be compared. They accommodate very different populations in terms of age, gender and the characteristics of their charges. One thing is clear, however. It cannot be claimed in terms of the subsequent lives and criminal behaviour of their charges that the SCHs or the STCs have a demonstrably better record than the Prison Service, but the institutions are not comparable. The SCHs tend to accommodate very young and damaged children whose behaviour is precociously serious, chaotic or out of control and for whom child protection issues, both in terms of their own self-harming behaviour and their vulnerability to family members and other adults, are often acute. There is a serious debate to be had about the proportion of young children in custody who might be dealt with through family as opposed to criminal proceedings and what alternatives, such as intensive fostering, might be employed as an alternative to custody. However, few commentators would doubt that for those very few young children whose behaviour, which sometimes includes murder or other acts of serious violence including arson and rape, requires their detention in a secure environment, specialist and other staff-intensive, child-centred provision is a necessity. Whether that provision goes under the label of 'welfare', 'penal' or 'psychiatric, it is always going to be very expensive.

In volume terms, the more pertinent questions concern those older adolescents, the overwhelming majority, in custody. Their placement is more obviously geared to a sentencing tariff. But it is highly questionable whether so many of these 15-, 16- and 17-year-old offenders need to be remanded in, or sentenced to, custody, following which the prognosis in terms of reoffending is relatively dire. Four out of five young prisoners are reconvicted – and it is important to emphasise that this is *not* reoffending but reconviction – within two years of release. If the young offender has many previous convictions (seven or more), he or she is virtually certain to be reconvicted (96%) and returned to custody (83%) within two years (Home Office, 2003, Table 9.10). There is no evidence that these statistics are improving. This is scarcely surprising given that, if the young people are still of school age, it is very difficult to get them back on a school roll or if, for whatever reason, they cannot return to their parental homes, many will end up in unsupervised bed and breakfast accommodation. Both situations are recipes for disaster.

Possible futures

In summer 2005, the YJB (2005) published its strategy for the future of the secure estate for children and young people. The document is both principled and pragmatic. The YJB describes the improvements that it considers have been achieved since 2000, yet acknowledges that 'there is still a long way to go' (YJB, 2005, para 2). It sets out its objectives, but concedes that the degree to which it will be able to realise its ambitions will depend on two factors: 'the sentencing trend' and the 'availability of resources', neither of which the Board has any control over and on which it exercises only limited influence. With respect to the first, as we have seen, the Board is failing. To what extent are the Board's objectives shared and what are the prospects of their being achieved?

The Board's vision is aspirational. It sets out principles with which few would be likely to disagree. For example, all secure institutions for children and young people should:

• have a child- and young person-centred culture;
• be run by staff committed to working with children and young people, who are adequately trained in this area of work, and who have completed nationally approved training in effective practice work with child offenders;
• have regimes that are fundamentally geared to the individual educational, training, recreational, cultural and personal developmental needs of children and young people and that are not disrupted by unnecessary transfers;
• employ an approach to behaviour management that emphasises, to the greatest possible extent, positive encouragement and reward rather than physical restraint or negative sanctions; and
• be located as close to young offenders' community ties as possible both in distance, and in terms of transport links and accessibility. (YJB, 2005, para 10)

But the principal arguments do not lie here. Rather they lie in the degree to which children are, in the first instance, held fully accountable for their behaviour in criminal law and, to the extent that they are held accountable, are dealt with by means of custody. What are the prospects for fundamental change in these regards?

The prospects appear poor. There is now so little political support for the change in direction adopted in many other European jurisdictions – raising from 10 the age of criminal responsibility and merging once again aspects of criminal and welfare legal proceedings, so that fewer children are dealt with by penal means – that most English critics have almost given up expressing their aspirations. It is left largely to international observers, from the United Nations to the Council of Europe, to express views that many leading members of the groups campaigning for children's interests hold but seldom now press. When the Council of Europe Commissioner for Human Rights recently commented adversely on the low age of criminal responsibility in England and Wales, and expressed surprise at the abolition of the doli incapax rule for children under 14 – a change he described as an 'excessive leap' – the government, in its response, did not even think it necessary to comment on his observations or his recommendation that the age of criminal responsibility be raised 'in line with norms prevailing across Europe' (Council of Europe Office of the Commissioner for Human Rights, 2005, paras 105-7).

The operational pressures resulting from the rising numbers in custody are unarguable. The YJB aims to have headroom in the number of places provided for children of 8 to 10%. This is necessary because some places are always out of commission for repair, redecoration or refurbishment and because there is always a degree of misalignment between the type or location of places provided and needed. The result, as we have noted, is that the Board is failing in its modest target of placing 70% of young offenders within 50 miles of their homes. The smaller the degree of headroom within the system, the greater the likelihood that children will have to be placed distant from home or in institutions less than ideal for them. To the extent that this happens, the greater the stresses on all concerned – the children, their families and the staff who work with them – and the greater the likelihood of self-harm and disorder. Further, the YJB estimates that some 200 to 300 older boys who 'require more intensive support than can currently be provided in YOIs' are nevertheless being so held (YJB, 2005, para 16). These include the young people who the YOTs have assessed as 'vulnerable', a term on which the Board considers it unsafe to rely because it is used insufficiently precisely. Nevertheless, as we have seen from the mental health and other characteristics of the population in custody, there are clearly many young offenders in custody who cannot adequately be cared for and safeguarded in the large YOIs by staff inadequately selected and trained for the purpose. The more the system is overcrowded, the greater the operational risks that things will continue to go badly wrong.

The YJB aims to reduce the courts' resort to custody primarily because it considers that, in most cases, reduced reoffending and public protection will in the long term be best achieved by greater reliance being placed on community-based measures. The Board aims to build the courts' confidence in these alternatives. However, it is significant, given the doubling of the custodial population since the early 1990s, that the Board aims to reduce the population by *only* 10%, and the fact that it feels that it is necessary to stress that this modest, and failing, target is 'realistic' reflects the mixed political messages that the government's policies have for youth crime levels and those agencies and decision makers who, cumulatively, determine the number of children in custody. On the one hand are the noble purposes set out in *Every child matters* and the 2004 Children Act (the five outcomes for children: 'being healthy'; 'staying safe'; 'enjoying and achieving'; 'making a positive contribution'; and achieving economic well-being' [HM Treasury, 2003, para 1.3]). On the other hand are the pressures created by the government's antisocial behaviour agenda, the focus of which is on young people (see Morgan, 2007; Waiton, 2008) and has been carried through with high-profile support from No 10, continued since Gordon Brown became Prime Minister (see Casey, 2008). It seems unlikely, therefore, whether reducing the juvenile population in custody will of itself become a high government priority.

This may, however, be too pessimistic a view. The fact that the new Department for Children, Schools and Families (DCSF) has since 2007 been wrestling with the new Ministry of Justice over the carcass of youth justice and the work of the YJB may signal a change of policy direction, with less emphasis being placed on criminal justice and more on children and young people's welfare needs. This stance is to some extent reflected in the interdepartmental 2008 Youth Crime Action Plan (YCAP) (HM Government, 2008). But, although general sentiments are expressed in the plan about building public confidence in preventive alternatives to criminal justice interventions in general and judicial confidence in sentencing alternatives to custody in particular, this is not the radical document that many observers had hoped for and it has little to say of a specific nature about custody. The future use of custody for children and young people remains uncertain, as does the organisation and financing of that provision.

References

Ball, C., McCormac, K. and Stone, N. (2001) *Young offenders: Law, policy and practice* (2nd edn), London: Sweet and Maxwell.

Carlile, Lord (2006) *The Carlile Inquiry: An independent inquiry into the use of physical restraint, solitary confinement and forcible strip searching of children in prisons, secure training centres and local authority secure children's homes*, London: The Howard League for Penal Reform.

Casey, L. (2008) *Casey Report: Engaging communities in fighting crime: A review*, London: Cabinet Office.

Coles, D. and Goldson, B. (2005) *In the care of the state? Child deaths in penal custody*, London: INQUEST.

Council of Europe Office of the Commissioner for Human Rights (2005) *Report by Mr Alvaro Gil-Robles, Commissioner for Human Rights, on his visit to the United Kingdom 4-12 November 2004*, Strasbourg: Council of Europe.

East Potential (2008) *Young offenders in east London: A new approach*, London: East Potential.

Galahad SMS Ltd (2004) *Substance misuse and the juvenile secure estate*, London: YJB.

Harrington, R. and Bailey, S. (2005) *Mental health needs and effectiveness of provision for young offenders in custody and in the community*, London: YJB.

Hazel, N., Hagell, A., Liddle, M., Archer, D., Grimshaw, R. and King, J. (2002) *Detention and training: Assessment of the Detention and Training Order and its impact on the secure estate across England and Wales*, London: YJB.

HM Government (2008) *Youth Crime Action Plan 2008*, London: COI.

HMIP (Her Majesty's Inspectorate of Prisons) (1997) *Young prisoners: A thematic review by HM Chief Inspector of Prisons for England and Wales*, London: HMIP.

HMIP (2003) *Annual report 2001-02*, London: HMIP.

HMIP (2004) *Annual report 2002-03*, London: HMIP.

HMIP (2005) *Annual report 2004-05*, London: HMIP.

HMIP (2007) *Annual report 2005-06*, London: HMIP.

HMIP (2008) *Annual report 2006-07*, London: HMIP.

HM Treasury (2003) *Every child matters*, Cm 5860, London: The Stationery Office.

Home Office (1997) *No more excuses – A new approach to tackling youth crime in England and Wales*, Cm 3809, London: Home Office.

Home Office (2003) *Prison statistics, England and Wales 2002*, Cm 5996, London: National Statistics.

Home Office (2007) *Sentencing statistics 2005 England and Wales*, Home Office Statistical Bulletin 3/7, London: Home Office.

Hough, M., Jacobson, J. and Millie, A. (2003) *The decision to imprison: Sentencing and the prison population*, London: Prison Reform Trust.

Howard League (2005) *Children in custody: Promoting the legal and human rights of children*, London: The Howard League for Penal Reform.

Labour Party (2001) *Ambitions for Britain: Labour's manifesto 2001*, London: Labour Party.

Labour Party (2005) *Britain forward not back: The Labour Party manifesto 2005*, London: Labour Party.

Ministry of Justice (2007) *Sentencing statistics 2006*, Statistical Bulletin, London: RDS NOMS.

Morgan, R. (2007) 'Children and young persons', in Y. Jewkes (ed) *Handbook on prisons*, Cullompton: Willan.

Morgan, R. and Newburn, T. (2007) 'Youth justice', in M. Maguire, R. Morgan and R. Reiner (eds) *The Oxford handbook of criminology* (3rd edn), Oxford: Oxford University Press.

Prison Reform Trust (2007) *Indefinitely maybe? How the indeterminate sentence for public protection is unjust and unsustainable*, Briefing paper, London: PRT.

Solomon, E. and Garside, R. (2008) *Ten years of Labour's youth justice reforms: An independent audit*, London: Centre for Crime and Justice Studies.

Waiton, S. (2008) *The politics of antisocial behaviour: Amoral panics*, London: Routledge.

YJB (Youth Justice Board) (2003) *Annual review 2002/2003: Gaining ground in the community*, London: YJB.

YJB (2004) *Annual review 2003/2004: Building in confidence*, London: YJB.

YJB (2005) *Strategy for the Secure Estate for Children and Young People*, London: YJB.

YJB (2007a) *Youth Justice annual statistics 2005/6*, London: YJB.

YJB (2007b) *Annual report and accounts 2006/7*, London: YJB.

YJB (2008) *Youth Justice annual workload data 2006/7*, London: YJB.

Types of secure establishment

2

Jim Rose

Introduction

While it is undoubtedly true that too many young people are in custody at any one time, for reasons that they present a 'danger to self or others', the use of secure accommodation is part of youth justice policy and is likely to remain so for the foreseeable future. If this is the case then there are decisions to make about what this should mean in terms of the circumstances in which young people are locked up and what kind of experiences are provided for them in the establishments where they serve their sentences. This chapter attempts to look 'under the skin' of the custodial regime and explore some of the critical factors influencing a young person's experience of custody and therefore its potential for providing positive experiences and opportunities for growth and development.

Background

The idea of a secure estate for children and young people is relatively recent and originates in the foundation of the Youth Justice Board (YJB) by the incoming Labour government in 1997. Since then, the YJB has been the main vehicle for the coordination of policy and practice across the whole youth justice system, with particular responsibility for raising standards in all types of custodial provision, in terms of both cost-effectiveness and regime provision.

Despite the structural and managerial changes of recent years, it is important to recognise the different historical traditions from which the present configuration of secure accommodation has emerged and to understand the impact that these have on the culture of individual establishments. The extent to which history shapes culture may be debatable; but, undeniably, the formal and informal narratives that make up the history of a particular establishment have a continuing part to play in the way that staff interpret their experiences and understand the establishment's role and purpose. This, in turn, impacts on the young people who pass through the establishment and contributes significantly to how they experience custody.

The history of residential childcare, the 'service' context for secure children's homes (SCHs), is quite different to that of young offender institutions (YOIs), which sit within the Prison Service and whose history is located within that of penal institutions. Secure training centres (STCs) are the most recent type of secure accommodation and were developed for the purpose of responding to a specific group of 'young persistent offenders', although their usage has become more generic under the stewardship of the YJB. To that extent, they represent something of a hybrid, designed specifically for a young offender population while including elements of practice more usual in children's services.

Of course, some cross-referencing is possible and necessary when thinking about the social, political and economic contexts in which these various forms of institutional care have developed over time. In general, however, there has been relatively little cross-fertilisation between these different strands of residential provision, and this remains the case despite the creation of the secure estate and the attempts by the YJB to develop a more coherent approach to performance management across the whole youth justice system. Such key areas as staff recruitment, training, supervision and management development remain noticeably discrete for each service, and there is little in the way of mobility of staff between the types of secure establishment.

However, trying to ensure a greater commonality between the different types of secure accommodation is not achieved simply by setting out common standards and procedures, useful as these may be. It depends on reaching a much more profound understanding about the purpose of secure accommodation and the kinds of approaches that are most likely to be effective in addressing the complex and multiple problems that are characteristic of young people sentenced to custody.

Who are the young people in custody?

The general conclusions of most surveys of the backgrounds and characteristics of the young people in all types of secure accommodation make salutary reading. Taking these findings into account is essential in planning relevant interventions and in shaping overall regime provision within which specific programmes are most effectively delivered. In summary, secure units:

> ... are dealing with young people who are likely to have had disrupted and disturbed experiences of family life from a very early age and many have been subject to various and often multiple forms of abuse by adults from whom they might have expected better. For a large number of these young people this has resulted in episodes of being in care, running away and fractured links with any form of stable home life. A significant number of the young people have had difficulties at school with both teachers and other children. This has resulted later on in either exclusion or truancy with the associated problems of having large amounts of unstructured time on their hands and contact with, or being influenced by antisocial peer groups. A high number have experimented with various forms of drugs or alcohol which in some cases means becoming dependent upon these substances. Many young people have long standing mental health problems and there are a significant number who have

Attention Deficit Disorder. A high percentage have attempted self harm and/or had suicidal thoughts and many have attempted to act on these. Young people in secure units may present with one, some or all of these problems in any combination, with varying degrees of severity and differences in age of onset. (Rose, 2002, p 33)

Organisation

In such a highly contentious area of social policy, and in an environment into which the full glare of media attention can be beamed when a serious incident occurs, a strong management structure that is supportive and understanding of the issues involved is essential. Ensuring a safe, stable and appropriately containing environment is a prime task for all those involved in the management of secure accommodation, not least for those who have external management responsibilities.

Young offender institutions

The creation by the Prison Service of a discrete juvenile estate carved out of the wider provision of young offender institutions (YOIs), along with the requirements for the delivery of a specific regime for 15 to 17 year olds, is enshrined in Prison Service Order 4950 (HM Prison Service, 1999). These establishments, of which there are currently 19, are generally large scale (300 plus places) and housed in Prison Service accommodation. The majority of the establishments are for boys, with separate and dedicated smaller facilities for older girls.

While there has been a considerable spend on facilities designed for the younger population, notably in education and health care, much of the estate consists of older buildings not built with any explicit purpose other than to house a prison population. The specific requirements that need to be considered, bearing in mind the needs of the young people described above, have not generally been addressed. With one or two exceptions, these are YOIs, often sharing a site and facilities with establishments for the older young offender population and remaining part of the Prison Service's regional management structure.

Despite attempts in recent years to develop alternative management for the juvenile estate, YOIs are now reincorporated into the general management arrangements that apply to all prisons. Line-management arrangements cannot therefore be specific to the circumstances relevant for the management of services for children and young people.

Secure training centres

The four secure training centres (STCs) are privately owned, built and run to specific contract specifications set out by the YJB. They are smaller than the establishments within the Prison Service estate, ranging from 40 to 80 places. The centres provide places for both boys and girls, and there is a dedicated unit for mothers and babies at one centre.

The ownership of these centres is highly complex and has changed over the years as a result of various mergers and takeovers among the larger companies, of which the STCs are subsidiaries. The 'parent' companies have diverse service portfolios across a range of security, penal and related areas of work. The nature of the contract arrangements varies across the different STCs, and the focus of external management is pretty much driven by the need to ensure compliance with the specific demands of the contract. As achieving compliance has financial implications in terms of possible penalties, this plays a significant part in the prioritising of issues.

Secure children's homes

Secure children's homes (SCHs), as these are now designated, are in the main owned and managed by the individual local authority within which they are located. There is some diversity in management arrangements, with involvement from the voluntary and private health care sectors for three of these homes. SCHs are smaller in scale than the rest of the secure estate, usually having between 16 and 32 places, and are built to higher specifications. There are establishments for boys and girls and also single-sex units.

Line-management arrangements for these units vary according to the particular structure of the managing authority. Although they are commonly located within the children's services directorate, the actual tier of management, where both the line manager and the manager of the establishment sit, varies considerably. The external manager is likely to have broad responsibilities across the service and the very specific demands that arise in managing secure facilities are often difficult to balance with the more general demands of children's services management. The situation is further complicated by the fact that SCHs not only provide places for young people remanded or sentenced under criminal legislation, but also accommodate those detained on welfare grounds under quite different conditions and for wholly different reasons.

Although common tasks can be identified for the 'external' managers of secure establishments – for example, performance monitoring – the fundamental purpose has to be to provide the staff and young people with a covering to contain the inevitable anxiety that arises from within the establishment and from outside agencies and the general public. This anxiety derives from the nature of the task, however it is defined: locking up children and young people whose delinquency and disturbance is troubling to society and about which there is frank ambivalence as to its meaning and about what responses are appropriate.

Staff

The internal structures across the three types of secure establishment are interestingly similar, although the nomenclature varies. There is a senior manager/governor in the YOIs, a director in the STCs and usually a principal or manager in the SCHs. In addition, there are several tiers of middle managers and teams of core residential staff who work with the young people on a daily basis.

With regard to the core residential staff, a further significant difference is in the ratio of staff to young people on duty at any one time. While it is not uncommon to have a ratio of four staff to eight young people in an SCH, on a prison 'wing' there may be four staff to look after up to 60 young people. This is not just about numbers but reflects a quite different understanding about the role of staff in terms of their expected relationship to the young people.

There are other professional staff who work in secure establishments, including teachers, psychologists, health workers, social workers and, usually on a sessional basis, psychiatrists. The numbers of these professionals available to an individual establishment vary, even within the discrete types of secure accommodation. In many respects the particular arrangements for the employment of these staff are incidental to the more critical question of how they are used within an establishment and their relationship to the management teams and core staff. Although there are issues about the training and support offered to these professional groups to prepare them for this type of work, their contribution is very much dependent on the internal culture of each establishment and the extent to which it is open to the particular knowledge and skills that they can bring to work with young people and to the support of residential staff.

The organisational context determines the key processes of recruitment, career progression and training for managers and residential staff within secure establishments. It may also be a decisive factor in determining the initial decision about which type of secure establishment to work in.

The governor of a YOI will certainly have a background in the Prison Service and may well have managed other types of prison before taking on responsibility for a juvenile establishment. Although, as governors, they will have been exposed to the issues of policy and practice that surround working with the younger population, they probably will not have a background in work with children and young people or experience of the broader range of services that exist for this age group.

On the other hand, the director of an STC is more likely to have a background in professional work with young people, although a closer look at the various appointments that have been made across this type of secure accommodation reveals an interesting range of experiences, including former prison governors, social workers and, for a short while in one establishment, an administrator!

The professional background and qualifications of the manager in an SCH will be located within the context of work with children and young people, with a likely base in social work.

The recruitment processes for residential staff in secure establishments are again determined by organisational context, and those applying to the Prison Service are not necessarily applying to work with young people, although this may become a later choice or preference. People applying to work in STCs at least know that they are applying to work with young people and this is also the situation for SCHs.

A general feature across all the types of secure accommodation is the profile of applicants; previous experience of work with children and young people is likely to be limited in all cases. However, those applying for work in SCHs may be more likely to be looking for a career in social work, while those applying to the Prison Service are likely to have different thoughts about career progression.

Perhaps of more significance than career aspiration is the nature and quality of the training that is offered to residential staff. The Prison Service introductory training is generic to work in the whole service and, while there are opportunities for more focused and specifically devised training in work with adolescents, these are necessarily limited.

The basic course for staff in STCs is of around six weeks' duration, while there is no specified induction period of training for staff coming new into the SCHs. However, it should be recognised that there are specifically designed programmes for SCHs, including induction, while the smaller scale of the operation potentially allows for more dedicated time to be allocated to staff training and supervision.

There are long-standing issues about the recruitment of staff to work in residential settings with children and young people that are not peculiar to secure accommodation. It is not clear that the YJB has managed to overcome these difficulties, certainly not to the extent of creating a common framework for recruitment to work in the secure estate.

The same sorts of conclusions may be drawn with regard to the issue of staff supervision and support. The work demanded of staff in these establishments is complex and difficult. Dealing with the daily management problems presented by young people in custody takes its toll on even the most experienced and highly qualified staff. The absence of a coherent model of supervision for Prison Service establishments is a major weakness in their ability to provide for this group of young people. While the other types of secure establishments acknowledge the need for structured supervision, it remains questionable whether any current provision is sufficient to address the real problems faced by staff and to offer the level of support they require.

Daily routines

The primary experience of young people in custody is in the daily routine of the living unit, whether that is on a wing in a YOI, or a unit in an STC or SCH.

Of course, the more formal aspects of the regime – attendance at education and related programmes to address offending behaviour or health issues, including alcohol and drug abuse – are important. However, research is consistent in showing that the ways in which the daily routines of residential living are provided and delivered by staff have the greatest impact on the young people and also influence their response to the more formal aspects of their programme (Liebling et al, 1999; Ashmore, 2000; Lyon et al, 2000).

By daily routine we are referring to the flow of the ordinary experiences of daily living: waking and getting up in the morning; mealtimes; the conversations and exchanges that occur in what have been described as the 'in-between times'; attending education and programmes; participation in leisure and recreation activities; and bedtimes. The interactions that accompany these events – between staff and staff, between young people and young people, and between staff and young people – provide the foundation for the overall experience and are crucial in determining outcomes.

These routines don't just happen. They require an understanding of their purpose and meaning by managers and staff, and the detail of the organisation to be structured around their reliable and consistent delivery.

In many respects, the daily routine as described looks the same irrespective of the type of establishment. The standards developed by the YJB have helped to ensure an overall commonality in how time is allocated: that is, the number of hours that young people can expect to be out of their rooms or cells and expectations about the education time available to each young person. Similarly, resources have been put in to try to equalise the quality of the provision available for education and healthcare in Prison Service establishments and other types of accommodation in the secure estate.

While it is true that the Prison Service has made great efforts to make the daily regime routines more appropriate for the younger age group, there are still a number of unresolved issues. In themselves, these might seem trivial, but they are actually quite significant: for example, the type of uniform worn by staff, the use of first names in addressing young people and the use of prison vocabulary to describe aspects of the regime. All of these things are essentially about what kind of ethos or culture is appropriate for establishments looking after young people, and in particular young people with the severity of problems facing those in custodial settings.

Given the nature of the difficulties experienced by the majority of young people in custody, the importance of the other more formal aspects of the routine is crucial. Reference has already been made to the increase in the educational opportunities provided across the secure estate, and there have been attempts to develop programmes to address offending behaviour, improve thinking skills and deal with issues of substance abuse. The introduction of the ASSET framework of assessment and the development of a standard screening tool for mental health have undoubtedly contributed to an overall improvement in the way these issues are responded to in all types of secure establishment. The fact remains, however, that it is the context in which these programmes are delivered and, crucially, the relationships that exist between staff and young people that determine their effectiveness in the longer term.

External agencies

Although it is the case that much of the energy and attention of those who work in secure establishments is directed at what is going on inside the unit at any one time, any measure of their effectiveness has to relate to what happens after the custodial period has been served. The capacity of an establishment to create and sustain good working relationships with wider family and professional networks for each young person is therefore critical. The prescribed frameworks that have been developed for sentence planning and case management have to be organised and delivered on a local basis. Both the YOIs and STCs have developed a model of casework teams, working alongside the core residential staff, but taking prime responsibility for communications with external agencies.

Issues such as geography – for example, the location of establishments, continuing pressure arising from the rising numbers of young people in custody and the varying sizes of the different types of secure accommodation – make it very difficult to establish the kind of ongoing relationships between the custodial sector and the Youth Offending Teams (YOTs) that might be desired. These pressures apply across the secure estate, but again there are issues of culture that impact. Although sentence planning has long been part of the prison officer's role, the more complex aspects of planning that are common in children's services are not easily assimilated. Although the casework teams help in this area, there is still the issue of how casework decisions are accommodated within the daily routine of the prison wing and understood by the core team of prison officers. This problem is not unique to the Prison Service (there have always been issues in residential work of how the wider staff team implements casework decisions), but the organisation in the other settings and the more generally focused approach to the needs of an adolescent group make it a more likely prospect that a consistent and well communicated approach will be achieved.

The same sorts of issues apply to the relationship between the establishments and the families of the young people. 'Visiting time' in a YOI is a different kind of experience for everyone compared with an STC, and even more so in the smaller, more informal setting that often exists within an SCH.

Towards a model of secure accommodation

Although the emphasis of this chapter has been on the ways in which different elements of certain key variables apply across secure establishments, there is another important question to ask: is it possible to draw together a coherent model for informing the work of managers and practitioners, which is sufficiently robust to satisfy the external agencies with responsibility for monitoring performance?

The starting point surely is to acknowledge the wide range of needs presented by young people in custody, not least those predicated by race and gender. In addition to these specific factors, however, consideration must be given to the chaotic family circumstances, low educational achievement and mental health difficulties that are characteristic of many young people in all types of secure accommodation.

Addressing these needs in a consistent and coherent way depends on having a clear set of ideas that inform daily practice and provide staff with ways of understanding the behaviours of the young people and the powerful feelings that are experienced when working with such delinquent and damaged groups. This is an area that is remarkably undeveloped across all the types of secure accommodation, despite recent advances in knowledge about the physiology of child and adolescent development and increased understanding of the importance of attachment and nurturing experiences to stimulate positive social and emotional growth.

It is in the context of this knowledge that the design of specific programmes to address offending behaviour and the problems of drug and alcohol abuse, as well as to provide opportunities to improve educational achievement, would seem to be most usefully set.

There are clearly many factors that have to be taken into account in defining model regimes for secure establishments. The recognition of the primary importance of the work of the core 'residential' staff in their day-to-day interactions with the young people is, however, central. This is highlighted in the Prison Service Order 4950 (HM Prison Service, 1999, 3.3.1) and summarised by Cosgrave (2000) who adds an important caveat:

The research shows that reinforcement and modelling of positive behaviours should be an important feature of work with young people. It further suggests that an effective pro-social modelling approach requires highly skilled staff, set in a context where work can be monitored. This work, while being the least visible, is in fact the most demanding, requiring constant vigilance, understanding and focus. Most of the day-to-day contact in secure facilities is by care staff or prison staff and, while many have excellent child care skills, this approach requires a more sophisticated level of knowledge and skill than generally they are expected to possess. (Cosgrave, 2000, p 1)

Conclusion

We have suggested a number of factors as essential for the delivery of an effective regime for young people in secure custodial facilities. These include: strong external and internal management arrangements that are able to provide essential containment and are supportive of the work of staff; properly recruited and well trained core staff teams, equipped with a working knowledge of the key ideas about the developmental needs of the adolescent group for whom they are caring and committed to positive, relational-based approaches in their day-to-day work with young people; properly coordinated use of staff from a range of professional disciplines who are integrated into the work of the establishment, supporting the core residential staff and offering targeted services to young people; well designed programmes that address the individual and assessed needs of each young person; effective casework systems that provide continuity between a young person's experience in custody and ongoing work in the community; and locally based provision that values and maintains family links for young people in custody.

Even this cursory review of current provision indicates that much is lacking in present custodial provision for young people. While it might be thought that the STCs offer the best hope, if only because of their intended singularity of purpose, the jury is still out in terms of the effectiveness of their regime and the outcomes they achieve for young people. The large number of young people continuing to be sentenced to custody means that there is little prospect of the Prison Service being phased out of what is arguably a specialist area of children's services, while economies of scale and high unit costs mitigate against SCHs in terms of offering a national provision.

The realities of the present situation with regard to available resources to cope with increasing demand for places can only be resolved by political decisions about the use of custody for young people. However, there is considerable scope to respond to some of the challenges outlined above: notably, to be clearer and more thoughtful about the underlying causes of the difficulties presented by young people in custody and to bring more appropriate focus to models of training and practice that are provided for staff.

The costs of secure accommodation cannot be measured solely in financial terms. There are human costs that ensue from the wasted potential of the lives of young people who, without skilled help and support, are likely to remain enmeshed in criminal activity. While the use of custody retains a role in the youth justice system, it is essential to ensure that the daily regime in every establishment offers each young person the appropriate level of safety, security and well-planned, positive experiences.

References

Ashmore, Z. (2000) 'A comparison of two secure regimes for male, juvenile offenders: measuring their performance', unpublished MSc thesis, Institute of Criminology, University of Cambridge.

Cosgrave, N. (2000) *Summary of effective practice*, London: Orchard Lodge.

HM Prison Service (1999) *Regimes for prisoners under 18 years old: Prison Service Order 4950*, London: HM Prison Service.

Liebling, A., Elliot, C. and Price, D. (1999) 'Appreciative inquiry and relationships in prison', *Punishment and Society: The International Journal of Penology*, vol 1, no 1, pp 71-98.

Lyon, J., Dennison, C. and Wilson, A. (2000) *Tell them so they listen: Messages from young people in custody*, London: Home Office.

Rose, J. (2002) *Working with young people in secure accommodation – From chaos to culture*, London: Brunner-Routledge.

3

The cost of custody: whose responsibility?

Rob Allen

Around the corner from the Home Office, in the wall of a building now occupied by the Royal College of Vets, is a foundation stone for Mr Fegan's homes. The House of Mercy was founded in the early part of the last century 'for the welfare of orphans, needy and erring boys'. Since then, erring boys (and girls) have increasingly been dealt with separately from those classed as needy – notwithstanding the fact that, in many cases, individual children fall into both categories.

The government changes of 2007, which restored to the department responsible for children's welfare a share in responsibility for youth justice in Whitehall, has reopened an important set of questions about agency responsibility for young offenders at the local level.

At the same time, there is a renewed and growing interest in how resources are used in the criminal justice system as a whole and whether increasing use of imprisonment represents a cost-effective response to crime. Government plans to spend £2.3 billion on capital costs for 10,500 new prison places by 2014 have begun to attract criticism, with the Justice Committee describing Lord Carter's report, *Securing the future,* upon whose conclusions the plans are based, as 'deeply unimpressive' (House of Commons Justice Committee, 2008a). The same committee has embarked on an inquiry into 'justice reinvestment', looking at the return for society of a policy of continued investment in prison building and other traditional methods of dealing with offenders (Allen and Stern, 2007).

These two strands of concern about responsibility and resources have served to ignite a particularly lively debate on the way we deal with juvenile offenders. There seems to be widespread agreement that there is too much use of both custodial remands and sentences, but strategies to reduce it have so far met with limited success. The Audit Commission's review of the reformed youth justice system in 2004 concluded that 'the most expensive and one of the least effective sentences is custody' and that the most persistent young offenders who might otherwise be sentenced to custody should receive an Intensive Supervision and Support Programme (ISSP) instead (Audit Commission, 2004, p 5). Among its recommendations, the Audit Commission suggested that Youth Offending Teams (YOTs) and courts should work to provide more feedback to high custody areas on the costs and the effectiveness of custody and community alternatives. The Public Accounts Committee, which considered the National Audit Office (NAO) report on the delivery of custodial and community penalties went further, suggesting that the Youth Justice Board (YJB) 'carry out an opportunity cost analysis of steadily moving part of the custodial places into effective community surveillance and supervision' (Public Accounts Committee, 2004, p 4).

In response to the stubbornly high rates of custody, there have been further calls in the run up to the publication of the Youth Crime Action Plan (YCAP) in July 2008 for changes to the way custodial placements are financed – in large part, to increase the incentives for local authorities and their partners to develop measures to keep children out of custody (Allen, 2006; PRT, 2008).

The YCAP does include some modest moves in this direction, placing new duties on local authorities to fund and commission education and training in juvenile custody, thereby for the first time bringing young offenders in custody under the education legislative regime. There is a commitment too to consult about making local authorities responsible for the full cost of court-ordered secure remand (rather than the one third cost they currently meet) and about ways of making the costs of custody more visible 'to help inform debate on whether, in the long-term, local authorities should be responsible for the placement and funding of custodial placements' (HM Government, 2008). But the government has made it clear that there are no current proposals to transfer child detention budgets to local authorities (*Hansard*, 2008a). It remains to be seen whether these proposals will be enough to satisfy the recommendation of a recent parliamentary committee that the 'Ministry of Justice should concentrate on finding mechanisms for driving down the numbers of young offenders in custody' (House of Commons Justice Committee, 2008a, p 75).

The aim of this paper is to describe the current responsibilities for meeting the costs of custody and discuss the likely impact of possible changes in the future.

The current arrangements

Custodial establishments for juveniles fall broadly into three categories: young offender institutions (YOIs), which form part of the Prison Service; secure children's homes (SCHs), largely run by local authorities; and secure training centres (STCs), run by private companies (see Morgan and Rose in this volume for further detail). A recent change to the law enables the Secretary of State to specify additional forms of accommodation in which young people serving a Detention and Training Order (DTO) may be placed, but the provision has yet to be implemented. There are also small numbers of young people held in secure accommodation in the health system whose costs are met by the NHS. But the vast majority of under 18s in custody are held in YOIs, SCHs and STCs.

Since 2000, the YJB has been responsible for commissioning and purchasing secure places for under 18s remanded and sentenced to custody by the courts. In 2007-08 the YJB spent £305.7 million on the purchase of secure places – 62% of its total budget and 65% of its youth justice programme expenditure (YJB, 2008, p 49). This compares with £279.2 million in the previous year (YJB, 2008, p 49) and £190.6 million in 2000-01 when its responsibilities in this area started (CCJS, 2008).

In 2007 the so-called secure estate comprised a total capacity of 3,545 places: 3,009 in YOIs, 301 in STCs and 235 in SCHs (*Hansard*, 2008b).

Young offender institutions

The YJB has a service level agreement with the Prison Service according to which an agreed number of places is provided to a negotiated regime specification. In 2007-08 the YJB spent £212.5 million on YOIs including escort costs (YJB, 2008). Almost all young people are allocated to one of 16 specific juvenile establishments or parts of establishments, although those classified as in need of maximum security can be held in adult prisons outside the secure estate. Of the 11 establishments where boys are held, four are for juveniles only. The remaining seven are so-called 'split sites', where young offenders aged between 18 and 21 are also accommodated. Two of the YOIs are privately run.

The Prison Service accounts make it difficult to assess the costs of YOI places for juveniles other than for the four male-only establishments. The accounts show that, in 2007-08, the cost per prisoner place in these varied from £34,373 at Wetherby to £45,634 at Werrington (Prison Service, 2008). The variation is largely explained by differences in staffing ratios. According to a parliamentary answer, at the end of March 2008, Werrington had 10 staff members for every 7.9 prisoners, while Wetherby had 10 for every 9.6. The cost per prisoner at Huntercombe, £37,322, was however higher than at Wetherby, although its staffing ratio was lower – 10 staff for every 12 prisoners (*Hansard*, 2008c).

The cost variation may also reflect different levels of education provided in the institutions, an element that is estimated to account for about 15% of the costs of YOIs (*Hansard*, 2007). A parliamentary answer revealed that, in 2007-08 at Werrington, juveniles spent on average 26 hours in educational activity per week, compared with 19.6 at Warren Hill, 16.9 at Huntercombe and 15.6 at Wetherby.

This is not the place for a wider discussion of the appropriateness of prison custody for juveniles but it is clear that, despite substantial investment in juvenile prisons, there is much to be done (Fayle and Allen, 2008). At the most basic level, recent inspections of juvenile establishments have shown the need for 'increased capital investment in an estate which is over-used, under-resourced and increasingly tired. Three older establishments were criticised for unsuitable or poor accommodation …

Reception environments, at the point where children are particularly vulnerable were often shabby, unwelcoming or too small' (HMIP, 2008, p 47).

Secure children's homes

The YJB contracts with 15 SCHs, spending just over £46 million in 2007-08. Apart from one unit, which has recently been taken over by the private sector, SCHs are run by local authorities and are subject to licensing and inspection by the Department for Children, Schools and Families (DCSF). Recent inspection reports by the Commission for Social Care Inspectorate have been very positive but, as a consequence of having the highest staffing ratios, the units are the most expensive in the estate and there is no coherent national strategy for funding them. YJB contracts are generally for short periods – three to five years. Responsibility for capital improvements rests with the DCSF.

SCHs play an important role in providing secure care for children who are not necessarily offenders but who need to be locked up for their own protection – often children who have run away from other placements. Local authority demand for welfare places has fallen in recent years, contributing to the closure of several units. At 31 March 2008, there were 340 approved places in the 19 SCHs open in England and Wales, a reduction of 10 homes since 2003 (DCSF, 2008).

Secure training centres

The YJB has been responsible for overseeing the contracts for the four STCs since 1 April 2000. The pricing mechanism is not based on the cost per young person, but on cost per available place. Detailed cost information is commercially sensitive, but the average annual cost of an STC place, excluding VAT, has risen steadily from £132,000 in 2000-01 to £149,000 in 2006-07. In 2007-08, the YJB paid a total of just over £47 million to the four STCs (*Hansard*, 2008d).

The private finance initiative (PFI) contracts for the STCs are much longer than the contracts with SCHs: 15 years in the case of Medway, Rainsbrook and Hassockfield and 25 years in the case of Oakhill. The contracts contain provisions for liquidated damages in the event of non-availability of places and failure to meet targets. These can and do provide a mechanism for resources to be returned to the YJB in the event of performance failure. The YJB does not set precise staff to prisoner ratios for STCs; instead, it agrees with providers the minimum starting levels necessary to ensure effective supervision. Broadly speaking, the minimum staffing levels are three members of custody staff to young people living in a group of eight and two members of custody staff to young people living in a group of six. It is estimated that 11% of the costs are spent on education (*Hansard*, 2008e).

Meeting the costs – the scope for justice reinvestment

Despite the complexity and variation in costs and financing arrangements between the three sectors, the position in respect of meeting those costs is more straightforward. When the court sentences a young person to custody, the costs of the placement are met by the YJB from the funds it receives from central government. This means that local authorities have nothing to lose financially when a custodial sentence is imposed. They may gain, in that costs that in some cases have been met by the local authority while the child is in the community – for example, for care or special educational provision – cease to be charged while they are placed in custody.

The basis of the justice reinvestment idea is that there is currently an incentive for 'cost shunting', in which local authorities fail to make interventions for which they have to pay, in the knowledge that, should the child offend, custodial costs will be met centrally (Allen, 2006). A small-scale research study on the use by local authorities of SCHs found 'little evidence' of cost shunting to the YJB or of the avoidance of decision making leading to an inappropriate reliance on the criminal justice system. However some young people ended up in secure placements in the youth justice system before a decision to apply to the court under the Children Act was made (Held, 2006). The former President of the Association of Directors of Children's Services told the Justice Committee that he did not accept the perverse incentive argument as something that 'happens in practice' (House of Commons Justice Committee, 2008b).

On the other hand, the Chair of the YJB told the Committee that 'if it is possible to find a way where local authorities feel the cost of the custodial places in the way they do not now then we would support that' (House of Commons Justice Committee, 2008b).

For court-ordered secure remands, there is a recognition that responsibility for meeting costs falls to both central and local government. A flat-rate Home Office contribution to the costs of the placing authority has been replaced by a system in which a third of the costs are met by the local authority in whose area the young person normally lives. The YCAP accepts that increasing the local contribution to costs 'would help local authorities make the case for investment locally in alternative forms of remand such as use of fostering' (HM Government, 2008).

There are a number of models for increasing local responsibility, but the purest form would see the whole of the secure budget transferred to local government, with local authorities having to purchase the places used for their children. Money saved by a reduction in use could be invested in the development of preventive programmes or community-based alternatives such as intensive fostering. This form of justice reinvestment has proved successful in reducing juvenile incarceration in Oregon (Tucker and Cadora, 2003).

There are two main questions that would need to be resolved if such a change were to be made. The first is how to find a fair way of allocating the budget currently held by the YJB, which introduced reasonable incentives to develop innovative ways of reducing custody. Should the allocation reflect recent patterns of custodial demand, potentially rewarding those who have made little effort hitherto and penalising low custody areas in, for example, the north east of England? Or should it seek to create an expected rate of custody, drawing on a wider range of data on offending and crime rates, deprivation and other social indices.

The second is to decide how far the local authorities' role would go in terms of purchasing and commissioning places. Would they themselves commission places or would there continue to be a need for a central body like the YJB both to manage the placement process and to oversee the hoped for downsizing of the secure estate? It would be important to ensure that a cost-driven process would not reduce standards and put at risk the safety and well-being of those children who did need to remain in custody. At the very least, some form of clearing house would be needed in respect of placements, but consideration could also be given to regional coordinating mechanisms in addition to or in place of the national one, currently the YJB.

The concern raised most often by local authorities relates to their ability to influence decision making. After all, decisions to remand or sentence children to custody are not made by them but by magistrates, judges and district judges. There is good evidence that the policy and practice of local authorities can influence the user of custody. Experience from the 1980s suggests that, by developing and advocating intensive and credible alternatives in appropriate cases, local authorities can make a substantial impact on the numbers of juveniles sentenced to custody (Allen, 1991). More recent evidence suggests that part of the explanation for the increasing use of custody in the last 15 years is that YOTs have been much more ready than they have in the past to propose sentences of detention in their pre-sentence reports for courts. It will of course be important that cost considerations do not mean that custody is never proposed as a matter of policy, and that courts are confident that costs are not exercising an inappropriate influence on recommendations.

The data suggest that YOTs should be capable of developing credible alternatives for many of those receiving short sentences – the 108 young people received under sentence for a month or less, the 239 received for three months or the 2,246 who were sentenced to between three and six months. They too should be able to create viable measures for some at least of the 120 young people in YOIs or prisons who were reported as being looked after by local authorities on 31 March 2007 (almost certainly an underestimate (DCSF, 2007)). A new localised funding system could, for example, encourage YOTs to put together 'hybrid' packages of intervention for persistent young offenders, which involved short periods in secure, semi-secure or open accommodation followed by intensive supervision (see Blyth and Newman in this volume). The current disincentive to offer such creative but relatively expensive solutions would be reversed if local authorities paid for custody as well as community programmes.

The main concern expressed about local authorities is whether they are up to assuming the responsibility. In a landmark ruling in 2005, Mr Justice Munby found serious shortcomings on the part of Caerphilly County Borough Council in the care of one of its children who had been sentenced to a DTO (*R [J] v Caerphilly County Borough Council*). If local authorities cannot meet their existing commitments to children for whom they have parental responsibilities, so the argument goes, how will they manage to deal effectively with serious and persistent offenders?

The quantum of funds involved should not in itself present a problem for local authorities. One comparator is provided by the Audit Commission study of pupils with special educational needs placed in out-of-borough schools, which found a total of 11,000 pupils educated in this way, more than half of whom were in residential placements. English councils spend about £500 million each year on these placements (75% of which funds residential placements) (Audit Commission, 2007). This compares with 7,097 custodial sentences and 6,360 custodial remands imposed by courts in 2006-07.

At the level of individual authorities too, the numbers of young people involved should not be unmanageable. In 2006-07, North Tyneside, whose use of custody was well below the national average, paid for 42 children to be accommodated in out-of-borough placements (Gollings and Watson, 2007). In that year, 28 custodial sentences and 22 custodial remands were imposed. Luton, an average user of custody, placed 38 children in out-of-borough placements, with 27 custodial sentences and 25 remands (Luton Borough Council, 2008).

The impact of moving the custodial budget to local government, and in effect seeing custody as a particular form of out-of-borough placement, would of course vary greatly between authorities. While the available data do not allow detailed cost profiles, it is possible to calculate the kind of sums likely to be involved if local authorities were to assume control for the funds currently disbursed by the YJB to pay for their children to be locked up. According to figures published by the Sentencing Guidelines Council (Sentencing Guidelines Council, 2008), children from Birmingham accounted in 2006-07 for 4.5% of custodial sentences and 5.7% of custodial remands. Assuming an average length of stay in the secure estate of 76 days and an average annual custodial cost of £90,000 per year, the city council could expect a budget of more than £10 million. Ceredigion, with two custodial sentences and one custodial remand in 2006-07, could expect well under £100,000.

More significantly, of course, the local authority areas with higher than average use of custody would stand to recoup and reinvest more by bringing down their rates. Merthyr Tydfil's 24 custodial sentences might cost only in the region of £500,000 but would free up £300,000 for reinvestment should the custodial sentencing rate in the borough (23% in 2006-07) fall to the average in England and Wales (9%).

Conclusion

Introducing a radical new way of financing custody for juveniles offers the prospect of substantial reductions in its use, something that other initiatives have failed to produce. There would of course be risks but also ways of mitigating these. The scheme could be piloted in certain areas or in respect of the youngest children. On 30 June 2008, of the 3,082 young people in custody, over half were 17. Limiting the localisation of budgets to those aged 15 or under (620 children) could provide a test bed for the new arrangements. Alternatively, the localisation could apply only to the DTO, thus insulating local authorities from the risk that a small number of very serious offenders for whom no alternative is really possible could produce excessive strain on a local custody budget.

While limiting the local responsibility in this way would meet some of the anxieties about the workability of a local approach, it might reduce the possible benefits. The Audit Commission report on youth justice in 2004 placed the issue within a larger framework of cost benefit:

> Many young offenders who end up in custody have a history of professionals failing to listen, assessments not being followed by action and nobody being in charge. If effective early intervention had been provided for just one-in-ten of these young people, annual savings in excess of £100 million could have been made. (Audit Commission, 2004)

Given local authorities' responsibilities for children in need, there is a strong argument that those in the criminal justice system should be brought more fully within their ambit. Many children in social, educational or mental health need for whom authorities and their local partners have existing responsibilities are exactly the same children who end up going to custody (Allen et al, 2007). Strengthening and integrating the preventive and rehabilitative response to this group of children across the age range and across their involvement with the state seems an obvious task for local government. Redeploying at least some of the budget currently used on expensive and often damaging placements in custody will play an important part in achieving that.

References

Allen, R. (1991) 'Out of jail: the reduction in the use of penal custody for male juveniles 1981-88', *The Howard Journal of Criminal Justice*, vol 30, no 1, pp 30-52.

Allen, R. (2006) 'From punishment to problem solving: a new approach to children in trouble', in Z. Davies and W. McMahon (eds) *Debating youth justice: From punishment to problem solving?*, London: Centre for Crime and Justice Studies, pp 7-54.

Allen, R. and Stern, V. (eds) (2007) *Justice reinvestment: A new approach to crime and justice*, London: International Centre for Prison Studies.

Allen, R., Jallab, K. and Snaith, E. (2007) 'Justice reinvestment in Gateshead – the story so far', in R. Allen, and V. Stern (eds) *Justice reinvestment: A new approach to crime and justice*, London: International Centre for Prison Studies, pp 17-34.

Audit Commission (2004) *Youth justice 2004*, London: Audit Commission.

Audit Commission (2007) *Out of authority placements for special educational needs*, London: Audit Commission.

CCJS (Centre for Crime and Justice Studies) (2008) *Ten years of Labour's youth justice reforms: An independent audit*, London: CCJS.

DCSF (Department for Children, Schools and Families) *Children looked after in England (including adoption and care leavers) year ending 31 March 2007*, London: DCSF.

DCSF (2008) *Children accommodated in secure children's homes at 31 March 2008: England and Wales*, London: DCSF.

Fayle, J. and Allen, R. (2008) 'Youth prisons no place for children', in *Children and young people now*, London: Children and Young People Now (www.cypnow.co.uk/Archive/login/779945/).

Gollings, A. and Watson, H. (2007) *Placement stability strategy/out of borough expenditure*, North Shields: North Tyneside Borough Council.

Hansard (2007) 17 December, Column WA112, London: The Stationery Office.

Hansard (2008a) 22 July, Column 1254W, London: The Stationery Office.

Hansard (2008b) 28 January, Column 150W, London: The Stationery Office.

Hansard (2008c) 28 April, Column 127W, London: The Stationery Office.

Hansard (2008d) 21 April, Column 1880W, London: The Stationery Office.

Hansard (2008e) 28 April, Column 126W, London: The Stationery Office.

Held, J. (2006) *Qualitative study: The use by local authorities of secure children's homes*, Research Report 749, London: DfES.

HM Government (2008) *Youth Crime Action Plan 2008*, London: COI.

HMIP (HM Inspectorate of Prisons) (2008) *HM Chief Inspector of Prisons for England and Wales annual report 06/07*, London: HMIP.

House of Commons Justice Committee (2008a) *Towards effective sentencing*, HC 184-I, Fifth report of session 2007-08 (vol I), Report together with formal minutes, London: The Stationery Office.

House of Commons Justice Committee (2008b) Uncorrected transcript of oral evidence taken before the Justice Committee inquiry on justice reinvestment, Tuesday 1 July.

Luton Borough Council (2008) *Performance Action Plan*, Luton: Luton Borough Council, http://agendas.luton.gov.uk/cmiswebpublic/Binary.ashx?Document=13651

Prison Service (2008) *Annual report and accounts 2007-2008*, London: The Stationery Office.

PRT (Prison Reform Trust) (2008) *Criminal damage: Why we should lock up fewer children*, London: PRT.

Public Accounts Committee (2004) *Youth offending: The delivery of community and custodial sentences*, London: PAC.

R (J) v Caerphilly County Borough Council (2005) EWHC 586 (Admin)

Sentencing Guidelines Council (2008) *The Sentence: The Sentencing Guidelines Newsletter*, no 8, January, London: SGC.

Tucker, S. and Cadora, E. (2003) 'Justice reinvestment', in *Ideas for an open society: Justice reinvestment*, New York: Open Society Institute, pp 2-5.

YJB (Youth Justice Board) (2008) *Annual report and accounts 2007/08*, London: YJB.

4

Sentencing young people

Kerry Baker

Introduction

> With those that like using custody, you can legislate till kingdom come and it wouldn't
> make any difference. (Parker et al, 1989, p 118)

The rise in the number of young people in custody in England and Wales is well documented (Bateman, 2005; Morgan and Newburn, 2007)[1] and it is also recognised that trends in sentencing are one of the key determinants of the custodial population (YJB, 2005). In considering the sentencing of young people there are three key areas of concern, namely: the level of custodial sentencing; the length and nature of custodial sentences (in particular, the new 'public protection sentences' introduced by the 2003 Criminal Justice Act [CJA]); and the extent of consistency or inconsistency in sentencers' decision making.

Given the range of factors contributing to the rise in the custodial population (Morgan, this volume) there is unlikely to be any single 'solution'. From their study of sentencing decisions in relation to adult offenders, however, Millie et al state that 'our findings suggest that the core of any strategy to reduce reliance on imprisonment … will be concerned directly with sentencing decisions, and in particular the decisions whether to imprison and how long to imprison' (2007, p 248). Clearly, neither the government nor youth justice practitioners can control sentencing trends, but they can, and do, try to influence them.

Current trends in sentencing policy and practice

The broad sweep of government sentencing policy has recently attracted some sharp criticism, including concerns expressed by the Lord Chief Justice about the 'politicisation of sentencing' (Judiciary of England and Wales, 2008) and an explicit statement from the House of Commons Justice Committee that the 2003 CJA had 'fallen short' of its aim to 'provide a coherent overall structure to sentencing in England and Wales' (2008, para 255). With this context in mind, this section looks at some of the specific concerns about sentencing in relation to children and young people.

---

[1] Other parts of the UK (for example, Northern Ireland) have significantly lower rates of youth custody.

Purpose(s) of sentencing

Recent legislation has attempted to clarify the purpose of sentencing with regard to young people. The 2008 Criminal Justice and Immigration Act (CJIA) states that courts must have regard to the principal aim of the youth justice system, which is to prevent offending and reoffending (s 9[2][a]). Courts must also have regard to the welfare of the offender in accordance with section 44 of the 1933 Children and Young Person's Act and in addition should take account of the following purposes of sentencing (s 9[3]):

- the punishment of offenders;
- the reform and rehabilitation of offenders;
- the protection of the public; and
- the making of reparation by offenders to persons affected by their offences.

What might be the impact of this new legislation? To begin on a positive note, is it possible that the new sentencing framework might prompt greater interest in the outcomes of custody for young people? Flood-Page and Mackie have argued that '[w]here the aim is to prevent reoffending – rather than simply to punish or protect the public – what is achieved by different sentences needs to be considered alongside costs' (1998, p 130). Thus, if the primary aim of sentencing for young people is to prevent reoffending, will we see government and/or sentencers taking a keener interest in recidivism rates for young people leaving custody?

On the other hand, this conflation of the different purposes of sentencing presents a number of problems. The provisions in the 2008 Act for young people are similar to those set out in section 142 of the 2003 CJA, which specified the purposes of sentencing for adult offenders. The obvious confusion that this creates – for example, different aims of sentencing can require contradictory actions – has already been clearly articulated (Ashworth, 2007). When applied to young people, this may add to the already existing tensions between the aim of preventing offending by young people generally (section 37 of the 1998 Crime and Disorder Act [CDA]) and the needs of individual young people. As Stone (citing Thomas, 1998) points out, if priority has to be given to preventing offending by young people generally, and not necessarily just by the individual offender being sentenced, courts may choose to impose custody as a deterrent penalty 'albeit one that does not serve the welfare and rehabilitation of that individual' (2001, p 43).

Intelligibility of the sentencing system

One of the most significant changes in recent years has been the introduction via the 2003 CJA of two new 'public protection sentences', namely (for young people) the 'extended sentence' and the sentence of 'detention for public protection' (see Sentencing Guidelines Council [2008] for full details of these sentences, including revisions made by the 2008 CJIA). The significant problems associated with these controversial sentences have been extensively discussed (Stone, 2006; Ashworth, 2007; Prison Reform Trust, 2007), one being that they are very complex to understand. The Court of Appeal stated this in fairly blunt terms:

> The fact that, in many cases, the sentencers were unsuccessful in finding their way through the provisions of this Act, which we have already described as labyrinthine, is a criticism not of them but of those who produced these astonishingly complex provisions. Whether now or in the fullness of time the public will benefit from sentencing provisions of such complexity is not for us to say. But it does seem to us that there is much to be said for a sentencing system which is intelligible to the general public as well as decipherable, with difficulty, by the judiciary. (*R v Lang and Others [2005]*)

Clearly, if the judiciary struggles to understand these legislative provisions then practitioners in Youth Offending Teams (YOTs) and the secure estate will also be perplexed, not to mention young people themselves, who may find it impossible to calculate, and thus work towards, a release date. This is clearly problematic because, if young people are to be successfully engaged in interventions (Mason and Prior, 2008), one of the key requisites is that they should understand the sentence and its implications.

Coming 'down the scale' to less demanding sanctions, will the introduction of the Youth Rehabilitation Order (YRO) following the 2008 CJIA make it easier or more difficult for young people to understand sentencing? Although the current plethora of disposals could be seen as confusing, it does at least allow for the idea of 'progression' from less to more serious sentences.[2] If this is replaced with a system in which young people can receive a series of YROs – albeit with potentially different components – will it be harder for them to realise how close they might be at a given time to the likelihood of a custodial sentence? Time will tell, but practitioners will need to be alert to the importance of explaining the new framework to young people.

'Hidden' consequences of sentencing

A degree of separateness from the adult criminal justice world has been an essential attribute of the youth justice system from its inception (Easton and Piper, 2005). More recently, however, there have been some indications that this sense of separation is being eroded. There are the obvious and well-known signs of this (such as the abolition of doli incapax in the 1998 CDA) but also some less immediately visible developments that seem to indicate a blurring of the distinction between adults

---

[2] For example, in ascending order of 'seriousness', there are Action Plan Orders, Supervision Orders, Supervision Orders with additional requirements and then custody.

and young people. That is, even in cases where the actual length of sentence may incorporate a 'discount for youth', young people are being drawn into adult-centric systems and procedures.

The public protection sentences introduced by the 2003 CJA are one example of this. Although the criteria for imposing an indeterminate sentence are different for young people than for adults, the impact is similar in that young people have to apply for parole in order to gain release and, despite recent moves to take more account of the specific needs of young people (Parole Board, 2008), the process remains essentially adult-centric (Kemshall, this volume). Multi-agency public protection arrangements (MAPPAs) are another example. A young person who has committed a sexual or violent offence listed in schedule 15 of the 2003 CJA and who receives a 12-month custodial sentence is classified as a 'category 2' MAPPA offender (see NOMS, 2007) and becomes subject to the same MAPPA processes as an adult, even if their sentence is substantially below that which an adult would have received for a similar offence. The 12-month sentence threshold is important therefore, not just in terms of the length of time for which a young person is incarcerated, but because it also then catapults them into other procedures where the distinction between adults and young people is, at best, somewhat blurred (Baker and Sutherland, forthcoming).

The sentencing decision

'Any attempt to change sentencers' decision-making will require a proper understanding of the decision process' (Hough et al, 2003, p 35). In trying to develop our conceptualisation of this process, it is helpful to identify the different elements of the decision-making process. These can include:

* how information is selected for, and presented to, the court;
* how sentencers sift and evaluate the credibility of information;
* how sentencers interpret information;
* sentencers' moral judgements about offenders;
* how sentencers make comparisons between different cases; and
* the use of sentencing guidelines or frameworks.

It is too easy to assume that sentencing is a techno-rational calculation that can be influenced with reasonable ease through measures such as sentencing guidelines and statements from government ministers. But, at each step in this process, there is room for factors such as personal bias or court culture to affect decisions and any attempts to influence sentencing practice need to take this into account.

There have been several studies in the UK of sentencer decision making with regard to young people who offend: for example, Parker et al (1989), Brown (1991) and, most recently, Solanki and Utting (forthcoming). Studies on sentencing practice in relation to adults include Flood-Page and Mackie (1998), Hough et al (2003), Tarling

(2006), Tombs and Jagger (2006) and Millie et al (2007). Within a short chapter such as this, it is possible to highlight only briefly some of the key themes emerging from the research and readers are encouraged to refer to the original material for further details.

Knowledge and attitudes

'Whether implicitly or explicitly, every sentencer operates with some ideology, some set of values, some penal philosophy' (McNeill, 2002, p 436). Unsurprisingly perhaps, the evidence seems to show that sentencers have mixed, and sometimes conflicting, attitudes. Solanki and Utting (forthcoming) found that sentencers were aware of how difficult custody could be for young people, but also that some still believed in the value of the 'short, sharp, shock' approach and others felt that custody could in some circumstances be of benefit to young people. In her study of one English local authority, Phoenix found that 'magistrates tended to view YOT information as biased (because it is "expert" knowledge and because YOT workers seldom recommend custody) and *privileged their own "common sense"* and observations' instead (2006, p 27, emphasis added). Thus, sentencers' beliefs and perceptions of their own expertise will influence decision making and may also affect the extent to which they follow or depart from sentencing guidelines.

Cultures and contexts

The powerful impact of local court cultures on sentencing practice has been identified in various studies (see, for example, Parker et al, 1989; Bateman, 2005) and is alluded to in the quotation at the beginning of this chapter. The other powerful contextual factor that must be taken into account is that of public opinion. Although public attitudes may not be as punitive as sometimes assumed (Hough and Roberts, 2004), the perception of the force of penal populism is relevant to understanding sentencing decisions. The extent to which sentencers say that they feel pressured by and/or take account of public attitudes varies (Millie et al, 2007), although it would clearly be difficult for it to be ignored altogether. It is of note that the House of Commons Justice Committee has criticised the government's handling of public debate on crime and called for a more 'informed and meaningful debate about sentencing policy' (2008, para 267).

Pre-sentence reports (PSRs)

There is an interesting question about the extent to which PSRs influence the sentencing decision. In their study of decisions made in 'cusp cases', Millie et al found that 'at least in borderline cases, the legal category of the offence with which someone is charged is not, as many might expect, the overwhelming determinant of the sentence. Instead, we found that other factors, and in particular factors related to offending history and personal mitigation, were at least equally influential' (2007: 260). If this is the case, then it might be thought that PSRs can have a strong impact on sentence (an argument supported by Bateman, 2005).

However, the evidence is not necessarily straightforward. Solanki and Utting (forthcoming) found that some sentencers reported that PSRs were of minimal influence in borderline custody cases, partly because YOT practitioners' reluctance to propose custody as a sentencing option meant that the reports lacked credibility. Such differences in the perspectives and philosophies of practitioners and sentences were one of the factors leading McNeill to argue that, with regard to reports designed to assist sentencing, 'the common sense association between quality and effectiveness remains open to question' (2002, p 445).

Services and resources

Evidence from studies in relation to adult offenders showing that sentencers did not routinely identify a lack of appropriate community provision as a factor tipping decisions towards custody (Hough et al, 2003) appears to be mirrored in recent research on young people (Solanki and Utting, forthcoming).[3] However, sentencers' perceptions of the quality of the provision may be more significant. Key factors emerging from research are that sentencing decisions are affected by the confidence that magistrates have in the local YOT (Bateman and Stanley, 2002) and by their perception of the quality of services provided (for example, their judgements about the rigorousness of supervision; see Moore et al, 2004).

Summary

This discussion has only skimmed the surface of the complexities of sentencing decisions but it nevertheless goes some way towards illustrating the claim that:

> The judge has to try and reflect, in each and every case, on a series of *conflicting* interests, purposes and concerns, and to form a judgement about the best answer to each individual case. It is ... rarely of easy application, but that is how the sentencing decision is made. (Judge, 2005, emphasis added)

---

[3] Although it should be noted that Solanki and Utting did report that sentencers were unhappy with the choice they faced in relation to first-time offenders, that is, the only available disposals were the Referral Order or custody. For this group of young people, sentencers wanted a wider range of non-custodial disposals.

Nowhere is this complexity more evident than in relation to the imposition of the new 'public protection sentences', in particular the indeterminate sentence of detention for public protection. We know little about the reasoning that lies behind the imposition of these sentences and research in this field would be an interesting and important addition to the current literature on sentencing decisions.

Understanding sentencing 'in action'

Even a brief overview such as this provides ample evidence in support of Tata's call for 'a greater awareness of the sociology of sentencing' (2002, p 4), given the obvious complexity arising from the interface of the broader policy trends and the factors that influence individual sentencing decisions. In trying to understand – and perhaps change – sentencing trends there is a need to look at the whole picture rather than isolated elements of the process.

Two examples can illustrate the point here. First, attempts to influence one goal may have different consequences from those intended or may conflict with other aims. For example, sentencing guidelines might increase the consistency of decision making and help to reduce some of the disparities noted in sentencing patterns (Bateman and Stanley, 2002), but they might also have the unintended outcome of shifting practice in a more punitive direction. It has, for example, been suggested that one factor contributing to why custody rates in England and Wales are different from those in Scotland has been the greater emphasis south of the border on the use of sentencing guidelines; these may have the effect of bringing 'lenient' sentencers closer to the practice of 'tougher' ones rather than the other way round (Millie et al, 2007). The impact of guidelines will depend on the surrounding political, social and organisational cultures but, as Millie et al state, '[w]hile there is no reason why guideline systems should inevitably have an inflationary impact, when they are introduced into sentencing systems that operate within a climate of penal populism, the likelihood of this occurring is clear' (2007, p 262). Demand for more guidelines or frameworks should therefore be tempered with an awareness of their possible disadvantages and their implementation monitored to assess impact.

The second example refers back to the earlier discussion regarding PSRs. As McNeill astutely shows, practitioners charged with writing PSRs (or social enquiry reports in Scotland) will have their own 'assisting sentence philosophy' of some kind (2002, p 436). As with sentencers, their decisions will be shaped by a variety of views, professional experiences and theoretical preferences. Report writers will also be affected by any prevailing policy confusion such that 'in a context where the purposes of sentencing are ill defined, the purposes of social enquiry must similarly remain unclear' (2002, p 444). It is not enough therefore just to give practitioners management guidance about PSRs (useful though this can be) without thinking through the context in which such reports are being written. This includes looking at the decision-making processes of practitioners who provide advice to courts as well as sentencers' responses to that advice.

Studies of sentencing often conclude with a list of recommendations (such as providing more information to sentencers about alternatives to custody), and this immediate practicality is perhaps understandable, particularly in the case of government-funded studies. There remains a need, however, for recognition that '[s]entencing is not so much a technical or value-neutral process as a value-laden process of constructing and exploring the narratives of the lives of the people in the dock' (Hough et al, 2003, p 39).

Conclusion

Trying to reduce imprisonment by altering sentencing decisions is not an easy strategy to pursue. To give a practical example, there is some evidence to suggest that this approach can often be associated with a redistribution of cases among non-custodial disposals rather than any significant reduction in the use of custody (McNeill, 2002; Ashworth, 2007). In addition, '[p]olicy discourse about sentencing generally fails to recognize the breadth of factors that currently feed into sentencing decisions' (Millie et al, 2007, p 261), which results in sometimes superficial policy initiatives. Third, the impact of changes in legislation on sentencing patterns is often limited:

> The experience of the 2003 Act also points towards the importance of not assuming that legislation is the only mechanism to achieve policy aims – it is only one tool and, in many cases, not the most appropriate tool. For example, the deficiencies in the 2003 Act illustrate the limited efficacy of legislation in bringing about cultural change such as a shift from the use of short custodial to community sentences. (House of Commons Justice Committee, 2008, para 259)

This is not to say that changes in these areas have no value. On the contrary, there are some recent welcome developments – such as the revisions to the criteria for imposing the extended and indeterminate sentences for public protection set out in the 2008 CJIA – which will be of benefit to young people. Rather, it is about being realistic and acknowledging the complexities of the sentencing process.

What will the future hold? There are a number of factors, such as the introduction of a YRO, the increasingly vocal campaigns from the children's rights movement and the effect of an impending economic downturn on public sector budgets, that could all affect the rate of custodial sentencing but whose influence is currently hard to predict. In terms of sentencing policy, the House of Commons Justice Committee has urged the government 'to address the welfare of young offenders as an explicit *purpose* of sentencing' (2008, para 229, emphasis added), although it is difficult to see any prospect of this being incorporated into legislation in the near future. The proposal for an 'enhanced Sentencing Guidelines Council' (Sentencing Commission Working

Group, 2008, para 9.7) looks more likely to be put into practice and this may lead to further guidelines, some of which would presumably apply to the sentencing of young people. A period of ongoing policy and legislative change looks inevitable and, in all of this uncertainty, there is thus a need for vigilance to maintain the distinction between adults and young people in both sentencing policy *and* practice.

References

Ashworth, A. (2007) 'Sentencing', in M. Maguire, R. Morgan and R. Reiner (eds) *The Oxford handbook of criminology* (4th edn), Oxford: Oxford University Press, pp 990-1023.

Baker, K. and Sutherland, A. (forthcoming) *Multi-agency public protection arrangements and youth justice,* Bristol: The Policy Press.

Bateman, T. (2005) 'Reducing child imprisonment: a systemic challenge', *Youth Justice,* vol 5, no 1, pp 91-105.

Bateman, T. and Stanley, C. (2002) *Patterns of sentencing: Differential sentencing across England and Wales,* London: YJB.

Brown, S. (1991) *Magistrates at work,* Milton Keynes: Open University Press.

Easton, S. and Piper, C. (2005) *Sentencing and punishment: The quest for justice,* Oxford: Oxford University Press.

Flood-Page, C. and Mackie, A. (1998) *Sentencing practice: An examination of decisions in magistrates' courts and the Crown Court in the mid-1990s,* Home Office Research Study 180, London: Home Office.

Hough, M. and Roberts, J. (2004) *Youth crime and youth justice: Public opinion in England and Wales,* Bristol: The Policy Press.

Hough, M., Jacobson, J. and Millie, A. (2003) *The decision to imprison: Sentencing and the prison population,* London: Prison Reform Trust.

House of Commons Justice Committee (2008) *Towards effective sentencing,* London: The Stationery Office.

Judge, Sir Igor (2005) The Atkin Lecture: 'The sentencing decision', www.judiciary. gov.uk/publications_media/speeches/2005/sp051125_1.htm

Judiciary of England and Wales (2008) *The Lord Chief Justice's review of the administration of justice in the courts,* London: The Stationery Office.

Mason, P. and Prior, D. (2008) *Engaging young people who offend,* Source Document, London: YJB.

McNeill, F. (2002) 'Assisting sentencing, promoting justice?', in C. Tata and N. Hutton (eds) *Sentencing and society: International perspectives,* Aldershot: Ashgate.

Millie, A., Tombs, J. and Hough, M. (2007) 'Borderline sentencing: a comparison of sentencers' decision making in England and Wales, and Scotland', *Criminology and Criminal Justice,* vol 7, no 3, pp 243-67.

Moore, R., Gray, E., Roberts, C., Merrington, S., Waters, I., Fernandez, R., Hayward, G. and Rogers, R.D. (2004) *National evaluation of the Intensive Supervision and Surveillance Programme: Interim report to the Youth Justice Board,* London: YJB.

Morgan, R. and Newburn, T. (2007) 'Youth justice', in M. Maguire, R. Morgan and R. Reiner (eds) *The Oxford handbook of criminology* (4th edn), Oxford: Oxford University Press, pp 1024-60.

NOMS (National Offender Management Service) (2007) *MAPPA guidance* (version 2), London: Ministry of Justice.

Parker, H., Sumner, M. and Jarvis, G. (1989) *Unmasking the magistrates: The 'custody or not' decision in sentencing young offenders*, Milton Keynes: Open University Press.

Parole Board (2008) *Parole for children and young people,* London: Parole Board.

Phoenix, J. (2006) *Doing justice: Analyzing 'risk' and 'need' assessments in youth justice practice*, London: Economic and Social Research Council.

Prison Reform Trust (2007) *Indefinitely maybe? How the Indeterminate Sentence for Public Protection is unjust and unsustainable*, London: Prison Reform Trust.

R v Lang and Others (2005) EWCA Crim 2864

Sentencing Commission Working Group (2008) *Sentencing guidelines in England and Wales: An evolutionary approach*, London: Ministry of Justice.

Sentencing Guidelines Council (2008) *Dangerous offenders: Guide for sentencers and practitioners,* London: Sentencing Guidelines Council.

Solanki, A.-R. and Utting, D. (forthcoming) *Fine art or science? Sentencers deciding between community penalties and custody for young people*, London: YJB.

Stone, N. (2001) 'Custodial sentencing: aims and principles in youth justice, disparity and other complexities', Legal commentary, *Youth Justice*, vol 1, no 3, pp 42-6.

Stone, N. (2006) 'Entering the labyrinth: sentencing the dangerous offender', Legal commentary, *Youth Justice*, vol 6, no 1, pp 61-9.

Tarling, R. (2006) 'Sentencing practice in magistrates' courts revisited', *Howard Journal*, vol 45, no 1, pp 29-41.

Tata, C. (2002) 'So what does "and society" mean?', in C. Tata and N. Hutton (eds) *Sentencing and society: International perspectives*, Aldershot: Ashgate, pp 3-39.

Thomas, D. (1998) *Annotations to Crime and Disorder Act 1998*, Current Law Statutes.

Tombs, J. and Jagger, E. (2006) 'Denying responsibility: sentencers' accounts of their decisions to imprison', *British Journal of Criminology*, vol 46, no 5, pp 803-21.

YJB (Youth Justice Board) (2005) *Strategy for the Secure Estate for Children and Young People*, London: YJB.

5

Child deaths in the juvenile secure estate

Barry Goldson and Deborah Coles

Introduction

This chapter engages with one of the most controversial issues in contemporary youth justice: child deaths in custodial institutions. The chapter maps recent trends in child imprisonment in England and Wales and reviews what is known about the biographies of child prisoners, together with the treatment and conditions that they experience within the juvenile secure estate. It presents an overview of 'safer custody' reforms and their limitations alongside a critical assessment of the investigation and inquest processes that typically follow child deaths in penal custody. We argue that knowledge of child deaths in the juvenile secure estate is conventionally fragmented and limited in scope. More recent recognition of the issues involved, however, has led to demands for closer scrutiny and public inquiry. Building upon this, the chapter concludes by summarising the case for comprehensive independent inquiry into child deaths in the juvenile secure estate and related questions of contemporary youth Justice policy.

Child imprisonment and child prisoners

England and Wales comprises one of the most punitive criminal justice jurisdictions in the modern world. In general, its level of imprisonment 'places it above the mid-point in the World List; it is the highest amongst countries of the European Union' (Walmsley, 2003, p 1). More specifically, greater numbers of children are imprisoned in England and Wales than in most other industrialised democratic countries in the world (YJB, 2004; Goldson and Muncie, 2006; Muncie and Goldson, 2006; Hazel, 2008; Muncie, 2008). Several commentators have detailed the dramatic expansion of child imprisonment over the last 15 years or so and there is little purpose in replicating such analytical accounts here (see, for example, Goldson, 2002a, 2006a, 2006b; Nacro, 2003, 2005). Perhaps most significantly, the pattern of penal expansion is seemingly unrelenting: 'the average number of children and young people in custody during 2007/08 was 2,942 – 196 more than in 2004/05, when the average was 2,746' (YJB, 2008, p 24). This all serves to impose serious pressure on the juvenile secure estate, which, according to Her Majesty's Chief Inspector of Prisons (2008, p 47), 'is over-used, under-resourced and increasingly tired'.

The consolidating pattern of penal expansion and the operational strain that it exacts are particularly problematic given the complex and pressing needs of child prisoners. Indeed, child prisoners are routinely drawn from some of the most structurally disadvantaged families, neighbourhoods and communities. Children for whom the fabric of life invariably stretches across poverty, family discord, state welfare, inadequate housing, circumscribed educational and employment opportunities, poor health and personal distress are the very children routinely found in penal institutions in England and Wales, as elsewhere (see, for example, Goldson, 2002b; Challen and Walton, 2004; Commission for Social Care Inspectorate et al, 2005; Mooney et al, 2007; Worsley, 2007; Prison Reform Trust, 2008). When the biographies of child prisoners are analysed 'it is evident that on any count this is a significantly deprived, excluded, and abused population of children' (Association of Directors of Social Services et al, 2003, p 6).

Concentrating excessive numbers of children with multiple needs into penal institutions that are experiencing substantial operational pressures is bound to give rise to serious problems. Her Majesty's Chief Inspector of Prisons (2008, p 48) observes bluntly that 'the basic needs of children are not properly met'. Indeed, the damaging and harmful excesses of child imprisonment are quite widely recorded, both nationally (see, for example, Children's Rights Alliance for England, 2002; Goldson and Coles, 2005; Carlile, 2006; Goldson, 2006c; House of Lords House of Commons Joint Committee on Human Rights, 2007; Coles et al, 2007) and internationally (see, for example, Gibbons and Katzenbach, 2006; Pinheiro, 2006; Detrick et al, 2008; Goldson, 2008).

Her Majesty's Chief Inspector of Prisons (2006, p 56) has reported that 'bullying remains a problem in most establishments'. The most obvious expression of bullying is physical violence, much of which goes unreported – thus unrecorded – owing to the intense antipathy to the practice of 'grassing' within 'inmate' culture and, worse still, the consequences of being labelled a 'grass'. Child prisoners are also exposed to many other forms of 'bullying', however, including: sexual violence; verbal violence (name-calling, threats, racist, sexist and homophobic taunting); psychological violence; extortion and theft; and lending and trading cultures, particularly in relation to 'canteen' and tobacco, involving exorbitant rates of interest that accumulate on a daily basis (Goldson, 2002b).

More controversially, institutionalised and officially sanctioned practices within child prisons in England and Wales, as elsewhere, frequently assume harmful forms. Her Majesty's Chief Inspector of Prisons (2008, p 48) has noted: 'Prison Service guidance on the use of force does not distinguish adequately between children and adults, or take into account child protection considerations'. This follows the Chief Inspector's earlier observation that 'injuries sustained during restraint are often the highest single category of child protection referrals in an establishment; but few properly monitor the injuries that arise from the use of force' (Her Majesty's Chief Inspector of Prisons, 2007a, p 41; see also Coles et al, 2007). Prison service statistics provided by the Youth

Justice Board (YJB) to an inquiry chaired by Lord Carlile of Berriew indicate that 5,133 'restraint' interventions were recorded in child prisons (young offender institutions [YOIs]) in England and Wales during the period January 2004 to September 2005 (Carlile, 2006, para 84). Furthermore, responses to parliamentary questions have revealed that 'restraint' was administered on 11,593 occasions in four private child jails (secure training centres [STCs]) between January 1999 and June 2004 (Carlile, 2006: paras 100-1). More recent figures show that, in the 10-month period between 1 April 2007 and 31 January 2008, 4,604 'restrictive physical interventions' were administered on children across the juvenile secure estate (Prison Reform Trust, 2008, p 23).

In addition to 'restraint', the officially sanctioned practices of strip-searching, 'sometimes carried out by force' (Her Majesty's Chief Inspector of Prisons, 2007a, p 41; see also 2008, p 48), placing children in segregation (solitary confinement) and denying children sufficient access to exercise and fresh air are also deeply problematic. The 'Carlile Inquiry' was informed that child prisoners were routinely required to submit to a full strip-search during their 'reception' to prison: 'this meant that one of the very first experiences for a child going into a prison was to be asked to strip and reveal their body to an unknown adult' (Carlile, 2006, para 154; see also Her Majesty's Chief Inspector of Prisons, 2008, p 18). Strip-searching takes at least two forms: upper body cavity searches, whereby prison officers check the child's ears, nose and mouth, and lower body cavity searches for which children are required to 'bend over or squat' (Carlile, 2006, paras 155-6). The 'Carlile Inquiry' (Carlile, 2006, para 207) also raised serious concerns about the use of segregation and solitary confinement units, prisons within prisons where children can be held 'for days and even weeks at a time'. Finally, at least for the purposes here, Her Majesty's Chief Inspector of Prisons (2007a, p 43) has reported that 'access to exercise in the fresh air remains a major concern. In our survey, only around half the girls and a quarter of the boys said they were able to exercise every day, and in one establishment, none said they were able to do so'.

Damage, harm and child prisoner deaths

For many child prisoners, the complex relation between structural and inherent vulnerabilities, their experience of being bullied, the practices of 'restraint', strip-searching and segregation, and the limits that are imposed on exercise and access to fresh air combine to perpetuate a profound sense of insecurity (Goldson, 2002b). Indeed, the treatment and conditions to which child prisoners are routinely exposed impose damage: be it emotional, psychological and/or physical. For some such prisoners the cumulative effect is too much to bear. Self-harm is not uncommon across the juvenile secure estate. In a period of just 11 months, for example, there were 1,324 reported incidents of self-harm in YOIs in England and Wales (Her Majesty's Chief Inspector of Prisons 2006, p 16). For such children, the pains of confinement are only relieved at the point of their release. For other child prisoners, 'release' takes a fatal form. Between July 1990 and November 2007, 30 children died in penal custody in England and Wales, 28 in prisons (YOIs) and two in private jails (STCs) (Goldson and Coles, 2005; Goldson, 2008; INQUEST, 2008a).

The limits of 'safer custody' reform

For many years – certainly since the revised 'suicide prevention' procedures came into effect in 1987 – the Prison Service has invested substantial time, effort and resources into 'safer custody' reforms. With specific regard to child prisoners, perhaps the single most significant reform has been the establishment of the YJB as provided by the Crime and Disorder Act 1998. Since its creation, the Board has endeavoured, along with its other duties, to apply 'safer custody' imperatives within the juvenile secure estate (YJB, 2004, 2007).

Taken in the round, the overall 'safer custody' reform agenda has been driven by the complex intersection of intra- and inter-agency reconfigurations, strategy documents, aspirational statements, official circulars, performance targets, inspections, audits and regularly updated operational policies, procedures and practices. Key highlights include: a Ministerial Roundtable on Suicide in Prisons; the establishment of a Prison Service safer custody group to operationalise a safer custody strategy; revised versions of Prison Service Order 2700 ('Suicide and self-harm prevention') and Prison Service Order 4950 ('Regimes for under 18 year olds'); the development of violence reduction strategies to counter inter-prisoner violence (particularly bullying); the appointment of suicide prevention coordinators in prisons; the creation of special projects to develop 'safer' prison design (including 'safer cells'); the introduction of practices and procedures to improve pre-reception, reception and induction processes (including health care and 'vulnerability' screening); the development of policies to facilitate more effective systems of intra- and inter-agency communication and information exchange; the establishment of refined allocation processes and placement strategies located within a 'comprehensive performance monitoring framework'; the implementation of more rigorous risk assessment and child protection policies, practices and procedures; the deployment of social workers within prisons; the implementation of 'safeguarding' arrangements linking child prisons with 'local safeguarding children boards'; and the application within prisons of specific provisions of the 2004 Children Act serving to impose legal responsibilities on governors to 'safeguard and promote the welfare' of child prisoners. Most recently, the Department of Health's Offender Health Group has issued a memorandum based on an analysis of 120 Prisons and Probation Ombudsman reports, in which it emphasises a number of 'safer custody' policies and practices including: continuity of care; rigorous information exchange; improved record-keeping; and integrated approaches to the care of prisoners (Department of Health, 2008). Furthermore, with specific regard to child deaths in the juvenile secure estate, the government has prepared a detailed 'comprehensive update on the continuing work being undertaken to reduce the number of deaths in custody' in which it claims 'substantial progress in a number of key areas' (House of Lords House of Commons Joint Committee on Human Rights, 2007, p 7).

It is not practical in a chapter such as this to undertake a detailed evaluative analysis of the above reforms. Besides, this has been attempted elsewhere (see, for example, Goldson, 2002b; Goldson and Coles, 2005). It is, though, important to acknowledge the limitations of such initiatives, together with the self-defeating challenges that confront them within the climate of penal expansion that we discussed earlier. The primary logic of 'safer custody' reform implies that harmful penal regimes can be 'cleansed' and the conditions that give rise to damage, and even death, can be 'designed out'. In the final analysis, however, there is no hard evidence to suggest that the innumerable policies, practices and procedures claiming to provide 'safe' institutional environments for child prisoners have ever succeeded or can ever succeed. As Jerome Miller wryly observed:

> Reformers come and reformers go. State institutions carry on. Nothing in their history suggests that they can sustain reform, no matter what money, staff, and programs are pumped into them. The same crises that have plagued them for 150 years intrude today. Though the casts may change, the players go on producing failure. (Miller, 1991, p 18)

Ultimately, and notwithstanding the best efforts of those involved, 'safer custody' or the 'caring prison' (Prisons and Probation Ombudsman for England and Wales, 2004, Ev 68) continues to elude child prisoners.

Fragmented knowledge

Despite the loss of 30 children's lives in penal institutions between July 1990 and November 2007, surprisingly little is known about child deaths in the juvenile secure estate, not least because of the limited scope of post-death inquiry. In cases where the police are satisfied that there are no grounds for prosecution (including self-inflicted deaths), at least two separate but related processes are conventionally activated. First, an investigation into the specific circumstances surrounding the child's death in the penal institution will take place. Second, the coroner's court (covering the geographical area within which the child's body is finally located) will be notified and the coroner will preside over an inquest. Official representations of such processes imply that they facilitate detailed scrutiny. In reality, however, the institutional framework within which post-death inquiry is located serves to limit the scope and depth of investigation and, as such, it tends to fragment knowledge.

With regard to investigations, and despite recent reforms, the disclosure of information remains conditional and the Prisons and Probation Ombudsman's investigatory function is exercised on a non-statutory basis. The office has no power to compel the production of evidence. Inquests have also been subject to recent reform, but they too remain seriously circumscribed in scope. The findings and recommendations reached by coroners and their juries following inquests into child deaths in penal custody are not routinely published. As such they cannot be systematically analysed, monitored or followed up. In practice, investigations and inquests effectively comprise 'a board game with a limited number of fixed moves'; a legal process that 'depicts a wholly non-pictorial world' (Cohen, 2001, p 108).[1]

Furthermore, traditionally there has been very little detailed research into child deaths in the juvenile secure estate. More recently, however, research – combined with substantial practical experience – has helped to identify a range of issues that consistently emerge with regard to child deaths in penal institutions, including:

- system strain (including overcrowding, hastily implemented and thus incomplete 'assessments', competing operational pressures that fundamentally compromise the 'duty of care');
- 'placements' in penal institutions that are not only unsuitable in nature but also inappropriate by location (exposing children to danger and rendering family visits near impossible);
- inadequate intra-agency and inter-agency communication and information exchange;
- problematic institutional cultures, operational regimes and practices (for example, bullying, strip-searching, restraint, solitary confinement in 'strip' [unfurnished] conditions, routine surveillance as distinct from watchful care);
- the damaging and harmful impact of penal custody on child prisoners;
- the institutional (mis)conceptualisation of genuine need as 'manipulation';
- persistent problems associated with the physical infrastructure of penal custody (including cell design and access to ligature points);
- inadequate medical care and limited access to specialist 'therapeutic' services (including child psychologists and adolescent psychiatrists);
- a failure to adequately implement 'suicide prevention' and child protection policies, practices and procedures; and
- ongoing deficits in terms of transparency, rigour and independent investigation that serve to impede learning and obstruct practice development (Goldson and Coles, 2005; Coles et al, 2007).

When the collective issues and the common characteristics of cases are collated and interpreted in this way, the conventional emphasis on *individualisation* and *exceptionalism* is rendered wholly inadequate. It is no longer possible to conceive of such deaths as isolated and unconnected aberrations. Indeed, at least in part, otherwise fragmented

---

[1] A detailed critical analysis of investigations and inquests relating to child deaths in penal custody is provided in Goldson and Coles (2005, pp 67-94). For a more general critique of the inquest process, see Scraton and Chadwick (1987); Thomas et al (2002); Liberty (2003).

knowledge begins to cohere and the consistent features and intersecting similarities of such cases reveal *systemic problems* and *institutionalised failings*.

Dawning recognition

The sheer scale of child imprisonment in England and Wales, the often harmful and damaging impact of penal regimes on children and, ultimately, the question of child deaths in the juvenile secure estate have, in recent years, prompted a sense of dawning recognition and developing critique. Major *systemic* problems have been identified by a wide range of authoritative sources including: international human rights bodies (see, for example, United Nations Committee on the Rights of the Child, 2002; Council of Europe Office of the Commissioner for Human Rights, 2005); parliamentary committees (see, for example, House of Lords House of Commons Joint Committee on Human Rights, 2003, 2004a, 2004b, 2005, 2007, 2008; House of Commons Committee of Public Accounts, 2004); independent inquiries (see, for example, Carlile, 2006); the High Courts (see, for example, Munby, 2002; Bennett, 2005; Buxton et al, 2008); state inspectorates (see, for example, Her Majesty's Chief Inspector of Prisons, 1997, 2006, 2007a, 2007b, 2008; Social Services Inspectorate et al, 2002; Commission for Social Care Inspectorate et al, 2005); independent researchers (see, for example, Goldson, 2002b; 2006a, 2006b, 2006c, 2008; Goldson and Coles, 2005; Detrick et al, 2008); state-sponsored researchers (see, for example, Challen and Walton, 2004; Holmes and Gibbs, 2004); penal reform organisations (see, for example, Nacro, 2003, 2005; Howard League, 2005, 2007; Prison Reform Trust, 2008) and non-governmental children's human rights agencies (see, for example, Children's Rights Alliance for England, 2002, 2007). More specifically, there has been a groundswell of support for a comprehensive independent inquiry into child deaths in the juvenile secure estate and this has been echoed in coroners' courts and in parliament.

On 30 April 2004, for example, the foreman of the jury at Shrewsbury Coroner's Court, recounting the verdict at the conclusion of the inquest into the death of Joseph Scholes, a 16-year-old boy who died just nine days into a custodial sentence at Stoke Heath YOI, announced:

> Our verdict is accidental death, in part contributed because the risk was not properly recognised or appropriate precautions were not taken to prevent it ... Do we consider that there has been *a failure in the system?* ... Yes, we do. (Cited in Goldson and Coles, 2005, p 107; our emphasis)

Moreover, the coroner himself concluded:

> I have powers under the Coroner's Rules to make recommendations and I am going to exercise that power in this case and I publicly announce now that I will be writing to the Home Secretary and I shall be writing in these terms. Not only should you

know that I am writing to him, you should know the substance of what I am writing to him and I am bringing to his attention the circumstances and issues arising out of the death of the late Joseph Scholes ... In all the circumstances, and so that the review can include *sentencing policy*, which is an essential ingredient but outside the scope of this Inquest, I consider that the review should take the form of a *Public Inquiry* when all interested persons can make their view known. (The coroner's concluding remarks at the inquest into the death of Joseph Scholes, Shrewsbury Coroner's Court, 30 April 2004, cited in Goldson and Coles, 2005, p 110; our emphases)

In 2007 further inquests were held into the deaths of two children detained in private jails (STCs). Gareth Myatt, who was serving a custodial sentence at Rainsbrook STC, died in April 2004, aged 15. Adam Rickwood, who was detained at Hassockfield STC, died in August 2004, aged 14, the youngest child ever to die in the juvenile secure estate (Goldson and Coles, 2005, pp 64-6; Coles et al, 2007, pp 21-9). In both cases the themes that emerged from the inquests 'paint a disturbing picture ... of repeated systemic failings' (Coles et al, 2007, p 29). Similarly, in February 2008, following the inquest into the death of 16-year-old Gareth Price who was found hanging in his cell at Lancaster Farms YOI in January 2005, both the coroner and the jury offered particularly detailed narratives within which *systemic* failings were again highlighted (INQUEST, 2008b).

Returning to Joseph Scholes, many MPs and peers have supported the call for a full public inquiry (INQUEST and Nacro, 2004) and, two months after the inquest, Chris Ruane MP tabled an Early Day Motion in parliament:

> [T]his House ... notes ... he [Joseph Scholes] was allocated to Prison Service accommodation without the standards of care needed for such a vulnerable child ... and therefore calls upon the Government to set up a comprehensive public inquiry to deal with the many issues concerning Joseph's death so that lessons can be learnt about the treatment of children in the criminal justice system. (Cited in INQUEST, 2004, pp 2-3)

The same month, June 2004, Lord Dholakia, supported by Baroness Stern and Baroness Howe, raised the matter in the House of Lords and, in December 2004, the Parliamentary Joint Committee on Human Rights not only acknowledged the substantial and authoritative push for a public inquiry, but also added further support:

> This is a call that we support. There has never been a public inquiry into the death of a child in custody. We recommend that the Home Secretary orders a public inquiry into the death of Joseph Scholes in order that lessons can be fully learnt from the circumstances that led up to his tragic death. (House of Lords House of Commons Joint Committee on Human Rights, 2004b, para 75)

Through such dawning recognition, it has become increasingly clear that 'an overall review of the use and type of youth custody is greatly needed' (Her Majesty's Chief Inspector of Prisons, 2008, p 49), and that such review will best be executed via comprehensive and fully independent inquiry.

A case for comprehensive independent inquiry

A key organisational mechanism for seeking truth, clarifying matters of accountability and, where appropriate, apportioning responsibility is the public inquiry. Public inquiries are a preferred method of systematically and comprehensively examining 'scandals' (Butler and Drakeford, 2003), they are more or less routinely opened with regard to complex cases of child abuse (Corby et al, 2001) and, of particular significance here, they have provided invaluable insights into the mistreatment of children in institutional settings (Kahan, 1994). In many such circumstances, public inquiries have led directly to major reforms in law, policy and practice. A conspicuous exception applies when the scandal, abuse and/or mistreatment might be located within a penal setting, however. There has never been a public inquiry into youth justice sentencing policy and/or the treatment and conditions endured by child prisoners in England and Wales. Perhaps more problematically, not a single public inquiry has been opened in respect of any of the 30 children who died in penal custody between July 1990 and November 2007.

As stated, significant support has developed for a comprehensive independent inquiry into child deaths in the juvenile secure estate, together with the wider policy and practice contexts within which such deaths are located. To date, successive governments have refused to allow such inquiry, however. Indeed, public inquiries are permissive and contingent upon governmental approval, and this, in itself, signals a key problem. Such inquiries conventionally offer no guarantees in terms of remit, powers, independence or effectiveness/impact. If the remit of the inquiry is restrictively defined, its full inquisitive potential will necessarily be diluted. If the inquiry is not empowered to compel the attendance of 'witnesses' then the depth and breadth of its investigatory reach will be further curtailed. If the chair of the inquiry is not truly independent and/or reluctant to exercise their power to the fullest extent, then the eventual inquiry report may comprise little more than 'whitewash'. Even if the inquiry is meticulously thorough, truly independent and underpinned by absolute integrity, government and state agencies are not statutorily compelled to act on its recommendations.

Despite apparent governmental resistance and the potential limitations of public inquiry, there is a compelling moral case for comprehensive independent inquiry into child deaths in the juvenile secure estate. To ensure that the nature and terms of such inquiry are unhampered by the confounds that can, in certain circumstances, afflict public inquiries, certain non-negotiable conditions might be applied. The scope of the inquiry should be wide-ranging under the direction of an authoritative chairperson of proven independence. The remit of such inquiry must necessarily embrace the cases of each and all of the 30 children who lost their lives between July 1990 and November 2007. While not neglecting the distinctive significance of individual cases, it must also seek to identify the commonalities within, across and between cases. The focus must also fix on youth justice policy in its broadest application and, more particularly, the statute and policies that govern the practices of child imprisonment. The inquiry should be empowered to subpoena witnesses and enforce the disclosure of all necessary documentation. In short, no stone should be left unturned.

In conclusion, the principal submission being advanced here is that only comprehensive independent inquiry will allow for the necessary lessons to be learnt and applied. To put it another way, it is only by implementing such inquiry that child deaths in the juvenile secure estate might finally be consigned to history.

References

Association of Directors of Social Services, Local Government Association and Youth Justice Board (2003) *The application of The Children Act (1989) to children in young offender institutions*, London: ADSS, LGA and YJB.

Bennett, The Honourable Mr Justice (2005) *Judgment approved by the court for handing down in R (on the application of Mrs Yvonne Scholes) v the Secretary of State for the Home Department*, 30 November and 1 December, London: Royal Courts of Justice.

Butler, I. and Drakeford, M. (2003) *Scandal, social policy and social welfare* (2nd edn), Bristol: The Policy Press.

Buxton, Lord Justice, Tuckey, Lord Justice and Keene, Lord Justice (2008) *Judgment approved by the court for handing down in R v the Secretary of State for Justice*, 16-17 July, London: Royal Courts of Justice.

Carlile, Lord (2006) *The Lord Carlile of Berriew QC: An independent inquiry into the use of physical restraint, solitary confinement and forcible strip searching of children in prisons, secure training centres and local authority secure children's homes*, London: The Howard League for Penal Reform.

Challen, M. and Walton, T. (2004) *Juveniles in custody*, London: Her Majesty's Inspectorate of Prisons.

Children's Rights Alliance for England (2002) *Rethinking child imprisonment: A report on young offender institutions*, London: Children's Rights Alliance for England.

Children's Rights Alliance for England (2007) *State of children's rights in England*, Number 5, London: Children's Rights Alliance for England.

Cohen, S. (2001) *States of denial: Knowing about atrocities and suffering*, Cambridge: Polity.

Coles, D., Khan, Y., Scott, M. and Dias, D. (2007) *INQUEST'S submission to the Ministry of Justice and Department for Children, Schools and Families on the 'Review of restraint'*, London: INQUEST.

Commission for Social Care Inspectorate, The Healthcare Commission, Her Majesty's Inspectorate of Constabulary, Her Majesty's Inspectorate of Probation, Her Majesty's Inspectorate of Prisons, Her Majesty's Crown Prosecution Service Inspectorate, Her Majesty's Inspectorate of Courts Administration and The Office of Standards in Education (2005) *Safeguarding Children: The second joint Chief Inspectors' report on arrangements to safeguard children*, London: Department of Health Publications.

Corby, B., Doig, A. and Roberts, V. (2001) *Public inquiries into abuse of children in residential care*, London: Jessica Kingsley.

Council of Europe Office of the Commissioner for Human Rights (2005) *Report by Mr Alvaro Gil-Robles, Commissioner for Human Rights, on his visit to the United Kingdom 4-12 November 2004*, Strasbourg: Council of Europe.

Department of Health (2008) *Common themes from analysis of 120 Prisons and Probation Ombudsman (PPO) reports*, Memorandum issued on 23 May, London: Department of Health Offender Health Group.

Detrick, S., Abel, G., Berger, M., Delon, A. and Meek, R. (2008) *Violence against children in conflict with the law; A study on indicators and data collection in Belgium, England and Wales, France and the Netherlands*, Amsterdam: Defence for Children International.

Gibbons, J.J. and Katzenbach, N. (2006) *Confronting confinement: A report of the Commission on Safety and Abuse in America's Prisons*, New York: Vera Institute of Justice.

Goldson, B. (2002a) 'New punitiveness: the politics of child incarceration', in J. Muncie, G. Hughes and E. McLaughlin (eds) *Youth justice: Critical readings*, London: Sage.

Goldson, B. (2002b) *Vulnerable inside: Children in secure and penal settings*, London: The Children's Society.

Goldson, B. (2006a) 'Penal custody: intolerance, irrationality and indifference', in B. Goldson and J. Muncie (eds) *Youth crime and justice: Critical issues*, London: Sage.

Goldson, B. (2006b) 'Fatal injustice: rampant punitiveness, child-prisoner deaths and institutionalised denial – a case for comprehensive independent inquiry in England and Wales', *Social Justice: A Journal of Crime, Conflict and World Order*, vol 33, pp 52-68.

Goldson, B. (2006c) 'Damage, harm and death in child prisons in England and Wales: Questions of abuse and accountability', *The Howard Journal of Criminal Justice*, vol 45, pp 449-67.

Goldson, B. (2008) 'Child incarceration: institutional abuse, the violent state and the politics of impunity', in P. Scraton and J. McCulloch (eds) *The violence of incarceration*, London: Routledge.

Goldson, B. and Coles, D. (2005) *In the care of the state? Child deaths in penal custody*, London: INQUEST.

Goldson, B. and Muncie, J. (2006) 'Rethinking youth justice: comparative analysis, international human rights and research evidence', *Youth Justice*, vol 6, pp 91-106.

Hazel, N. (2008) *Cross-national comparison of youth justice*, London: YJB.

Her Majesty's Chief Inspector of Prisons (1997) *Young prisoners: A thematic review by HM Chief Inspector of Prisons for England and Wales*, London: Home Office.

Her Majesty's Chief Inspector of Prisons (2006) *Annual report of HM Chief Inspector of Prisons for England and Wales, 2004-2005*, London: The Stationery Office.

Her Majesty's Chief Inspector of Prisons (2007a) *Annual report 2005/06*, London: The Stationery Office.

Her Majesty's Chief Inspector of Prisons (2007b) *Report on an announced inspection of the management, care and control of young people at Oakhill Secure Training Centre*, London: HMIP.

Her Majesty's Chief Inspector of Prisons (2008) *06/07 HM Chief Inspector of Prisons for England and Wales annual report*, London: The Stationery Office.

Holmes, C. and Gibbs, K. (2004) *Perceptions of safety: Views of young people and staff living and working in the juvenile estate*, London: Her Majesty's Prison Service.

House of Commons Committee of Public Accounts (2004) *Youth offending: The delivery of community and custodial sentences*, Fortieth report of session 2003-04, London: The Stationery Office.

House of Lords House of Commons Joint Committee on Human Rights (2003) *The UN Convention on the Rights of the Child*, Tenth report of session 2002-03, London: The Stationery Office.

House of Lords House of Commons Joint Committee on Human Rights (2004a) *Deaths in custody interim report*, First report of session 2003-04, London: The Stationery Office.

House of Lords House of Commons Joint Committee on Human Rights (2004b) *Deaths in custody*, Third report of session 2004-05, London: The Stationery Office.

House of Lords House of Commons Joint Committee on Human Rights (2005) *Government response to the third report from the committee: Deaths in custody*, Eleventh report of session 2004-05, London, The Stationery Office.

House of Lords House of Commons Joint Committee on Human Rights (2007) *Deaths in custody: Further developments*, Seventh report of session 2006-07, London: The Stationery Office.

House of Lords House of Commons Joint Committee on Human Rights (2008) *The use of restraint in secure training centres*, Eleventh report of session 2007-08, London: The Stationery Office.

Howard League for Penal Reform (2005) *Children in custody: Promoting the legal and human rights of children*, London: The Howard League for Penal Reform.

Howard League for Penal Reform (2007) *Children in prison: An independent submission to the United Nations Committee on the Rights of the Child*, London: The Howard League for Penal Reform.

INQUEST (2004) *INQUEST's further evidence to the Joint Committee on Human Rights September 2004: Deaths in custody – The current issues*, London: INQUEST.

INQUEST (2008a) *Deaths of children in penal custody (England and Wales) 1990-date*, London: INQUEST.

INQUEST (2008b) *Damning critical verdict at inquest into the death of 16 year old Gareth Price*, Press release, 20 February, London: INQUEST.

INQUEST and Nacro (2004) *Why are children dying in custody? Call for a public inquiry into the death of Joseph Scholes*. London: INQUEST and Nacro.

Kahan, B. (1994) *Growing up in groups*, London: HMSO.

Liberty (2003) *Deaths in custody: Redress and remedies*, London: The Civil Liberties Trust.

Miller, J. (1991) *Last one over the wall: The Massachusetts experiment in closing reform schools*, Columbus, OH: Ohio State University Press.

Mooney, A., Statham, J. and Storey, P. (2007) *The health of children and young people in secure settings: Final report to the Department of Health*, London: Thomas Coram Research Unit, Institute of Education, University of London.

Munby, The Honourable Mr Justice (2002) *Judgment approved by the court for handing down in R (on the application of The Howard League for Penal Reform) v the Secretary of State for the Home Department*, 29 November, London: Royal Courts of Justice.

Muncie, J. (2008) 'The "punitive turn" in juvenile justice: cultures of control and rights compliance in Western Europe and the USA', *Youth Justice*, vol 8, pp 107-21.

Muncie, J. and Goldson, B. (eds) (2006) *Comparative youth justice: Critical issues*, London: Sage.

Nacro (2003) *A failure of justice: Reducing child imprisonment*, London: Nacro.

Nacro (2005) *A better alternative: Reducing child imprisonment*, London: Nacro.

Pinheiro, P.S. (2006) *World report on violence against children*, Geneva: United Nations.

Prison Reform Trust (2008) *Bromley briefings prison factfile*, London: Prison Reform Trust.

Prisons and Probation Ombudsman for England and Wales (2004) 'Memorandum from Prisons and Probation Ombudsman for England and Wales', in *House of Lords House of Commons Joint Committee on Human Rights Deaths in custody interim report*, First report of session 2003-04, London: The Stationery Office.

Scraton, P. and Chadwick, K. (1987) *In the arms of the law: Coroners' inquests and deaths in custody*, London: Pluto.

Social Services Inspectorate, Commission for Health Improvement, Her Majesty's Chief Inspector of Constabulary, Her Majesty's Chief Inspector of the Crown Prosecution Service, Her Majesty's Chief Inspector of the Magistrates' Courts Service, Her Majesty's Chief Inspector of Schools, Her Majesty's Chief Inspector of Prisons and Her Majesty's Chief Inspector of Probation (2002) *Safeguarding children: A joint Chief Inspectors' report on arrangements to safeguard children*, London: Department of Health Publications.

Thomas, L., Friedman, D. and Christian, L. (2002) *Inquests: A practitioner's guide*, London: Legal Action Group.

United Nations Committee on the Rights of the Child (2002) *Committee on the Rights of the Child, thirty first session: Concluding observations of the Committee on the Rights of the Child: United Kingdom of Great Britain and Northern Ireland*, Geneva: OHCHR.

Walmsley, R. (2003) *World prison population list* (5th edn), Findings 234, London: Home Office.

Worsley, R. (2007) *Young people in custody 2004-2006*, London: HMIP and YJB.

YJB (Youth Justice Board) (2004) *Strategy for the Secure Estate for Juveniles: Building on the foundations*, London: YJB.

YJB (2007) *Update on the Strategy for the Secure Estate for Children and Young People,* London: YJB.

YJB (2008) *Annual report and accounts 2007/08,* London: The Stationery Office.

6

Sentenced to education: the case for a 'hybrid' custodial sentence

Maggie Blyth and Robert Newman

The seamless sentence: making the link between custody and community

For many practitioners and policy makers embracing the youth justice reforms in 1998, the potential for integrating education into offending behaviour work through the new Detention and Training Order (DTO) introduced by the 1998 Crime and Disorder Act was greatly welcomed. Nearly all of the young people who have received a custodial sentence since 2000 have had DTOs that require the first half of the sentence to be served in custody and the last half in the community imposed by the courts. The minimum length for DTOs is four months and the maximum is two years. Young people on DTOs are held in one of three types of institutions: young offender institutions (YOIs); secure training centres (STCs); or secure children's homes (SCHs). The majority are held in the Prison Service environment of a YOI.

The Youth Justice Board (YJB) revised its vision for custody over three years ago, setting out a commissioning framework for the newly named Secure Estate for Children and Young People (YJB, 2005a). In the early days of the DTO, there was an assumption at a local level among youth justice specialists that the multi-agency work to be brokered by Youth Offending Teams (YOTs) with education departments would improve young people's access to mainstream education. At national level, there was a commitment from policy makers that the new custodial sentence would locate education at the heart of all sentence planning, enabling much more effective work to be undertaken with young people in custody to address both protective and risk factors. Indeed, the early evaluation of the DTO (YJB, 2002) was broadly positive, indicating that the sentence was well received by sentencers and practitioners. A number of recommendations were highlighted, and the researchers emphasised that crucial planning and resettlement work failed where interventions were dependent on agencies immediately outside the YOT. Clearly, education provision was one key area that appeared to break down fairly rapidly and, despite much effort over the years since 2002, little improvement has been made. Following this work, the Audit Commission highlighted in some detail the continuing problem of young people not gaining access to suitable education, training and employment (ETE) opportunities. It was critical of the way in which local education authorities and schools relinquished their commitment to young people once they entered custody and recommended that schools should retain responsibility for young people in custody and that the funding should follow the child (Audit Commission, 2004, Recommendation 5).

This chapter will explore the continuing limitations of the DTO nearly a decade into the youth justice reforms, looking broadly at the extent to which access to education remains an outstanding problem for most young people sentenced to custody. Within this context, a case will be made for reviewing the purpose of the DTO, emphasising its link to education provision, while examining current policy changes within children's services and the 14-19 education framework that may facilitate any evaluation of the DTO. With the development of early intervention, targeted provision and the raising of the statutory school age, careful consideration should be given to a new hybrid sentence that places education firmly at its centre. For the purpose of this chapter, we have decided to call this the Education Placement Order (EPO).

What are the links between education and youth offending? Is there an evidence base?

In preventing offending, the reformed youth justice system under the direction of the YJB has placed great emphasis on the importance of young people participating and progressing in education. Although the causal links between education and offending behaviour are complex, there has been some work, largely commissioned by the YJB since 2001, demonstrating that absence from mainstream education and educational underachievement are linked to crime (YJB, 2008a). There is a body of evidence that shows the links between non-participation in education and subsequent delinquency (Hayward et al, 2004; in particular, Stephenson, 2007). A study of risk and protective factors associated with youth crime found considerable overlap between risk factors for youth offending and those for educational underachievement (YJB, 2005b).

The recognition of the existence of a NEET (not in education, employment or training) population and national targets aimed at reducing NEET figures locally have been important steps forward in holding local authorities to account for those children most at risk from detachment from education. A significant number of young people contained within any NEET population will be young people who offend and, for this reason, YOTs have been working at a local level to focus on interventions that improve learning and increase school participation. This has not been easy, and engagement with children's services remains patchy across the country, as can be evidenced from the difference in performance across YOTs in meeting the YJB target to ensure that 90% of young offenders are in suitable full-time education, training and employment at the end of their orders. The most recent data show the proportion nationally of young offenders in ETE remains on a plateau of under 70%, and nearer 50% for the DTO cohort, after some improvement between 2004 and

2005 when the target was first established (YJB, 2007). Significantly, this indicator, specifically related to young people in the youth justice system, has been included among the 200 new local area agreement indicators following the local government performance management reforms. This must be seen as vindication of the YJB's use of an education engagement measure as a vital contributor to reducing reoffending.

Performance in relation to education in the secure estate has been measured differently, with establishments required to provide specific hours of education. A review of the National Specification for Learning and Skills across the secure estate for children and young people, undertaken by ECTOEC for the YJB in 2005 (YJB, 2005c), indicated that performance varied considerably across establishments and with individual young people. Similarly, targets to improve the literacy and numeracy levels of incarcerated children and young people have had mixed results. In YOIs, the latest figures for 2006-07 show that only a third of young people have improved their basic skills while in custody (Solomon and Garside, 2008; YJB, 2008b).

It is therefore striking that, despite the potential of the DTO to assist young people to improve their educational attainment, it has had very little impact on basic educational outcomes for young people and very little effect on reducing reoffending. However, if the opportunity provided by a more coherent 14-19 framework, including all children and young people, is utilised in the secure estate, there is, for the first time, the real prospect that an effective model could be designed at local level to meet the needs of young offenders both in custody and in the community.

Moreover, there is also now an emerging evidence base within youth justice, based on research, to support the idea of identifiable critical components for any education programme aimed at the most detached young people. The strands are likely to include:

- the use of mainstream environments, principally further education (FE) colleges, to dilute delinquent peer group effects and promote behaviour modification;
- intensive supervision, supported by the YOT;
- multi-modal approaches that focus on offending behaviour as well as education; and
- a high degree of programme intensity (Stephenson, 2007, p 192).

There must be opportunities for realistic progression, especially in basic skills and increased employability. The YJB has developed enrichment programmes over the last five years, largely in the arts, and these components would be a necessary part of any curricula, properly accredited and linked to mainstream provision.

Reviewing the DTO

The fact that most of the problems associated with the early evaluation of the DTO remain unresolved is frustrating. There has been an acknowledgement that there are significant shortcomings surrounding current resettlement arrangements for young people leaving custody (YJB, 2002; HM Government, 2008). The YJB itself recognises that, despite its aspirations and those of practitioners working in youth justice services, the DTO is not yet providing the 'seamless' transition between custody and community (Audit Commission, 2004). The latest workload data from the YJB indicate that, in relation to both the sustained resettlement of young people back into the community and to any meaningful reduction in recidivism, the outcomes are questionable (Solomon and Garside, 2008; YJB, 2008b).

Reoffending rates among the juvenile population remain high, with just over 67% of young people sentenced to custody reoffending (YJB, 2008b). For young people sentenced to custody, most are on relatively short sentences, with the average time spent in custody being four months. This leaves barely any time to assess young people's needs and plan any rigorous intervention, particularly where there are special learning requirements. Information exchange and paper flow between community and custody has continued to be a challenge and, although e-links are now established between the secure estate and YOTs, ASSET information remains generally poor across some YOTs (YJB, 2005c; HM Inspectorate of Probation, 2006). Young people are commonly subjected to different assessment frameworks and very few secure establishments would gain critical information contained in a Common Assessment Framework (CAF) or Special Educational Needs (SEN) assessment, where relevant. This level of information exchange would be considered unacceptable within the community and it is reassuring that new measures outlined in the Youth Crime Action Plan (YCAP) will address these problems.

Although the YJB has oversight of all individual placement decisions in the secure estate, the pressure on the system, exacerbated by high custodial demand, has resulted in young people being transferred across the country at regular intervals and being placed far from home and local communities, with additional concerns highlighted over safeguarding (see Goldson and Coles in this volume). The links between families and children are therefore weakened and any effective case planning with wider children's services becomes virtually impossible, particularly where YOT staff members are themselves struggling to maintain crucial visits to young people dispersed in institutions across England and Wales. The consequences of the churn across Prison Service establishments, in particular, has led to children and young people being transferred more than once during sentence and has disrupted all attempts to sustain effective learning environments (YJB, 2005c).

There appears to be, on the available evidence, a considerable problem for many young people sentenced to DTOs in avoiding further reoffending. In light of the inherent shortcomings of the DTO, this chapter considers whether the time may now be right to revisit the way we sentence young people and asks the difficult question about whether a sentencing structure based on the adult criminal justice model is necessarily the best approach to rehabilitating young people. The changing direction of youth justice services, with an emphasis on prevention and rehabilitation alongside enforcement, with greater oversight by children's services, provides a coherent backdrop for any re-evaluation of the fitness for purpose of the DTO in reducing reoffending among children and young people.

The notion of the EPO, placing young people in an educational setting for an agreed period of time, is not radically new, but it may well be that, as the reformed youth justice system comes under fresh scrutiny (HM Government, 2008; Solomon and Garside, 2008), the merits of an intensive residential educational option for young people at risk can be trialled. A new order that focuses primarily on education as a means of rehabilitating those young people whose criminal behaviour is deemed out of control and requires removal from the community could have considerable scope for reducing offending and is likely to be more cost-effective than current arrangements (see Allen in this volume).

There is no scope within this chapter to examine the extent to which the EPO should be 'secure', as opposed to merely residential. Moreover, there is no question that the secure estate would reduce available placements for those young people perceived as 'dangerous' or requiring detention for public protection issues. For the purpose of this chapter, we concentrate on the EPO as a new type of hybrid order, sitting alongside the DTO, targeting those young people whose behaviour places them at risk of further serious offending and who require intensive monitoring within a residential setting. Eligibility for an EPO is considered later in the chapter.

This proposal for a new hybrid sentence, the EPO, comes at a time when the government has announced its 'triple track approach' to tackling youth crime. The benefit of a cross-government analysis of youth offending is that the issue of shared responsibility for young people in the youth justice system is now being seriously reconsidered. The model is replicated at a local level where YOTs straddle the gap between children's services and correctional agencies.

This chapter will examine a number of interlocking factors arising from recent policy now supporting the case for a review of the DTO, with a view to identifying those young people who might benefit from a different type of educationally based order. For the purposes of this chapter, these factors have been divided into three main themes: the development of children's services and the emphasis on early intervention; the implementation of the 14-19 education agenda and new duties on local authorities to incorporate offender education in custody; and, finally, important sentencing changes now enshrined in legislation, most notably the new Youth Rehabilitation Order (YRO).

1. Children's services and early intervention

It has been noted that both the Youth Taskforce Action Plan and the YCAP published during 2008 are important milestones in establishing the direction of youth justice services for the next three years (DCSF and DIUS, 2008; HM Government, 2008). The two documents extend the Every Child Matters agenda firmly into the territory of early intervention, providing a new framework at a local level for targeted prevention work with young people and their families. There is an expectation that the work of YOTs will become more integrated into children's services, with evidence already that some YOTs across the country are merging formally with new targeted youth support services to provide an integrated model for early intervention. In Nottingham, where the YOTs and youth services have already merged, the city has been identified as the first UK 'early intervention city', backed by ministers, with the following definition, intended to enable all partner agencies to work closely together with those young people who find themselves in trouble:

> Our aim is to break the intergenerational nature of underachievement and deprivation in Nottingham by identifying at the earliest possible opportunity those children, young people and families and to intervene and empower people to transform their lives and their future children's lives. (One Nottingham, 2008)

In targeting services and considering the needs of children and young people who offend within the wider context of children's services, there is scope for ensuring that any criminal justice intervention is supported adequately by programmes that reduce risk. This should apply equally to any custodial sentence but will work only if there are clear strategic links between services provided in custody and local partnerships within children's services. With significant funding for preventive work that also supports enforcement of antisocial behaviour measures, announced by government in the Children's Plan and YCAP (DCSF, 2007; HM Government, 2008), there are new requirements on local agencies to take more responsibility for children and young people who offend under clearer governance arrangements with children's services alongside Crime and Disorder Reduction Partnerships. YOT management boards must ensure that these governance arrangements are formalised with the necessary strategic partnerships at local level, with outcomes measures prioritised through local area agreements. Indeed, the statutory governance of YOT boards is an area the government wishes to strengthen.

Government plans for young people who offend place emphasis on targeted work with families and an extension of parenting programmes, holding parents to account for criminal behaviour. In their joint introduction to the YCAP, key ministers outline their plans for a 'comprehensive cross government analysis' of youth crime with a section on custody that aims to change behaviour, improve educational attainment and prepare young people for resettlement into the community (HM Government, 2008). The extension of family intervention work, and recognition that young people's risk factors must be addressed alongside wider family issues, is essential in ensuring that partnership agencies work together to ensure the effective resettlement of young people into the community on release from prison.

The renewed statements indicating the importance of resettlement are encouraging. Currently, the second half of the DTO can be fairly ineffective, with high levels of breach and around 50% of young people not in full-time education, training or employment at the end of their sentence (YJB, 2008b). For those young people, already disadvantaged and detached from mainstream services, including education, the custodial element can compound the situation. The high turnover of custodial placements, especially in the larger institutions, provides infertile ground for planting the seeds of effective resettlement.

The YCAP provides the framework for improving the resettlement of young people from custody as well as the education they receive while in custody. The proposed new duties for local authorities should result in greater local responsibility for ensuring that services to young people in custody are a clear priority for children's planning. The government has acknowledged in the YCAP that the centralised custodial commissioning system developed by the YJB over the last decade has done little to reinforce any ownership at local level for the young people sentenced or remanded into custody. This is further evidence supporting the case for a hybrid order over which children's services, alongside the YOT, are in the driving seat.

2. Education: raising expectations

During 2007, the government consulted widely on education for young people supervised by the youth justice system in England, with a particular focus on the needs and outcomes of young offenders of compulsory school age, through a series of issues papers (DfES, 2007). This signalled a recognition that young people in the youth justice system were disproportionately marginalised from mainstream education provision. It also appears to complement the shift in emphasis to early intervention and prevention, as local authorities become accountable for the commissioning and funding of education and training for all young people through the 14-19 agenda (DCSF and DIUS, 2008). Consistent with this message is the new duty to be placed on local authorities to include within this cohort those young people in custody (HM Government, 2008). The government offers two options for funding arrangements within this new model of local authority led delivery of education.

One model is for the 'host' local authority to be responsible for planning and arranging education in custody, regardless of where the young people held there have come from. This model is consistent with wider proposals for mainstream provision post-16. However, this model provides little incentive for 'home' local authorities (where the young people are from) to maintain an interest in young people's education while they are in custody.

An alternative model is for the host local authority to be responsible for planning and arranging education in custody, but for home local authorities to be responsible for funding education for young people from their areas. This would involve host local authorities recouping the cost of education from the young people's home local authorities.

The latter model is considered to have the important advantage that the home local authority remains financially responsible for the young person's education, regardless of where the young person is placed in the custodial estate. This could create strong financial incentives for home local authorities both to prevent young people from entering custody in the first place and to maintain a role in ensuring appropriate education. There are, however, practical difficulties in its implementation, which may well result in the host local authority funding and commissioning education against a nationally agreed framework, with the home local authority given more comprehensive duties as set out in the YCAP for the ongoing engagement of the young person through a number of measures similar to those now in place for 'looked after' children.

The thrust of these recommendations is fleshed out in more detail in recent work entitled 'Justice revisited' (Allen, 2008; Allen in this volume). Clearly, as the government attempts to make the cost of custody more visible at local level, local authorities may eventually have to contribute to the direct cost of a young person entering custody.

The changes to the overall planning, commissioning and funding of 14-19 education directly support the notion of the EPO. With the greater accountability of local authorities to consider and resource quality provision for *all* young people within a geographical area, for the first time this will also include those young people within the secure estate for children and young people as part of 14-19 arrangements. Where in the past some local authorities would have shown little interest in the education of their children in custody, there is now an opportunity to engage those responsible for 14-19 planning with education provision in secure settings. Where children are now taken off the school roll when a custodial sentence is imposed, there may well be greater flexibility in the future for the funding to accompany the child to a secure setting, with emphasis on linkage to mainstream curricula and additional support located for special learning needs. Where workforce issues have compounded poor quality education in secure settings in the past, the 14-19 planning framework provides an opportunity to look at quality issues across the board, including higher standards of teacher recruitment and training, with the potential for post-qualifying teachers to gain necessary work experience in secure settings. The focus of the Department for Children, Schools and Families (DCSF) in concentrating on attainment, increased achievement and realignment with mainstream provision for all children and young people indicates that any education provided in a secure setting would be expected to meet the quality framework proposed by the government for all 14-19 education and the requirements of the government's Children's Workforce Strategy. The new diploma structure also provides the necessary components of vocational education required by many secure establishments and so is supported by the relevant inspectorate (HMIP and YJB, 2005). The plans to raise the education participation age to 18 mean that, in the future, any 'sentenced to education' provision could be applied to the older age group without significant legislative change. Closer links between secure establishments and the Connexions Service are perhaps more viable as these services were drawn into children's services planning from April 2008.

3. Sentencing and criminal justice legislation

The changes to the placement definition in the 2007 Offender Management Act mean that the DTO can now be served in a variety of other 'non-custodial' settings. The legislation relaxes the requirement for the accommodation in which the DTO is served to be necessarily for the purpose of restricting liberty (Offender Management Act, 2007: Explanatory Notes 144/5).

Simultaneously, the new YRO, to be implemented through 2009, outlined in the 2008 Criminal Justice and Immigration Act, augments the rehabilitative elements attached to a community order with an emphasis on access to mainstream services. This may enable additional conditions to be attached to the community element of any new hybrid order to focus on education, training and employment, working alongside the Connexions Service and Job Centre Plus.

The new purpose of the sentence enshrined in the YRO is helpful, that is: first, to prevent offending (or reoffending); second, to consider the welfare of the offender; and, third, to consider the purposes of sentencing, that is, punishment, reform and rehabilitation, protection of the public and reparation to persons affected by offences (2008 Criminal Justice and Immigration Act, part 2, s 9). The idea of a menu of rehabilitative interventions has to be viewed as a positive step forward in terms of maintaining public confidence while providing sentencing flexibility. Yet for some young people, without residential structure, the YRO interventions may not be intensive enough or may lack the necessary resourcing to be implemented effectively. Certainly, the Intensive Supervision and Surveillance Programme (ISSP), the only current community package with robust intensive requirements, has demonstrated that young people require significant additional support to be able to maximise educational opportunities and sustain attending any programme (YJB, 2004). Participation in an EPO through residential requirements might provide that extra structure to help some young people refrain from further offending and avoid permanent detachment from the mainstream.

Characteristics of a 'hybrid' sentence

Clearly, as outlined earlier in this chapter, there is an emerging education evidence base about what works with young offenders, and this should form the basis of any

EPO (Stephenson, 2007; YJB, 2008a). However, in determining the characteristics of the EPO, there is an argument for pitching the length of the order and the type of placement on the basis of the educational and personal development needs of the young person, the home circumstances and the justification for removal from home and community. The notion of sentencing based on 'needs' as well as 'deeds' is already enshrined within the government's cross-government analysis on youth crime (HM Government, 2008). Clearly, any proposals must be based on a proper risk assessment, taking into account public protection considerations. Time for planning entry into the placement could be built into the EPO, based on a contract negotiated with the young person, their family and selected education provider. This would overcome the problem of placement without adequate preparation that currently affects the custodial system. The EPO itself would be supervised by the YOT in line with National Standards for Youth Justice, and breach of the order, triggered by repeated absconding or the committing of further offences, could lead to the imposition of a more conventional custodial sentence. Equally, the EPO could provide the resettlement part of any earlier custodial sentence to ensure a more staged release into the community and return to mainstream education. To avoid the disruption caused by current short DTO sentences, it would be sensible to encourage much longer EPO orders, of between one and two years, in order to ensure that the educational and personal development gains required to impact on offending behaviour could actually be delivered. Review of the order complements government plans to take high-risk cases back to court at regular intervals to enable sentencers to monitor progress (HM Government, 2008).

Eligibility and funding

Earlier attempts to reduce the use of custody through the provision of robust community interventions, most notably the ISSP, have been questionable in terms of actually reducing the use of custody (see Morgan in this volume). While a hybrid order with a residential component might be suitable only for a small proportion of the current custodial population, certainly those eligible for intensive fostering, these would generally be young people under the age of 16 years currently occupying expensive SCH or STC places, and the order could also provide the resettlement element of the DTO where the risks of reoffending were felt to be high enough to merit it. There would also be a significant number of young people who exhibited high reoffending risk factors but had not yet served a custodial sentence for whom the EPO would prevent the otherwise inevitable future custodial sentence. Between these two groups, it is likely that there would be sufficient numbers to justify the commissioning of placements from existing residential education providers. In general, specialist residential education placements are considerably cheaper than an SCH placement, so there is a sustainable argument that such an approach could have an impact on both improving recidivism rates and educational attainment at a reduced cost. Information from the Independent Schools Council (ISC) suggests that the average cost of a residential special needs placement is in the region of £55,000 per year. This compares with the projected average costs of an SCH placement of £195,000 per year anticipated for 2008-09 (YJB, 2007).

There is an historical precedent for attempting to harness the rehabilitative powers of education in reducing delinquency, with both borstals and approved schools preceding community homes with education (CHEs) in 1969. When the 1982 Criminal Justice Act replaced borstals with youth custody this signalled the end of any pretence that detention would in future be education led until the arrival of the DTO under the 1998 Crime and Disorder Act. The current political climate and the reorganisation of 14-19 education under local planning arrangements with accountability for offender education provide a fresh perspective for assessing the effectiveness of secure settings and the relationship between education and youth crime. With a well-developed provider base for residential services ranging from therapeutic communities, through schools for young people with emotional and behavioural problems, to the 'mainstream' independent sector, there are available resources and interested providers available. And, arguably, it is within this sector that the largest skill base of teachers and residential workers, experienced in working with some of the most difficult and challenging young people, is located.

Conclusion

From punishment to problem solving is the title of a 2007 report on youth justice services, which argues that both the DCSF and children's services should lead on arrangements to tackle head on the problems faced by many children and young people in the youth justice system in lieu of the punishment-only approach (Allen, 2007). In keeping with this sentiment, the cross-departmental action plan on youth crime suggests that government has heard the message, albeit with some further work to do.

This chapter has aimed to demonstrate that the early intervention approaches led by children's services, coupled with greater duties on local authorities to take charge of education for all 14-19 year olds, provide the necessary backdrop for reviewing the DTO and its fundamental links to education. However, whether this policy landscape reflects an actual sea change in government policy on youth custody remains to be seen. A number of themes stand out.

First, it is imperative for YOTs to work closely with children's services to implement the government's action plan on youth crime and harness opportunities arising from early intervention approaches. If young people in the youth justice system are not prioritised and custody is seen as a convenient means of removing difficult young people from local communities then the current custodial trajectory is likely to continue. Second, there is a danger that, although local authorities will take responsibility for the planning and commissioning of offender education, conflicting resource priorities will reduce the likelihood of quality curricula being available in secure establishments and the education focus of both the custodial and community elements of the DTO will be hindered. Third, in the current political climate of harsher custodial sentences for young people who commit crime, there may be reduced interest in exploring other residential orders for young people that may appear less focused on enforcement.

If the government is serious about both reducing the reoffending of young people coming out of prison and improving their educational outcomes, there is merit in capitalising on the 'three track approach' that current wider government policy offers for young people at risk, looking at how services are configured and who is held accountable for what happens to young people during and after sentence. A review of the DTO and consideration of the potential contribution of a residential Educational Placement Order goes a long way along this road.

References

Allen, R. (2007) *From punishment to problem solving*, London: Centre for Crime and Justice Studies.

Allen, R. (2008) 'Justice reinvestment. A new approach to crime and justice', *Prison Service Journal*, no 176.

Audit Commission (2004) *Youth justice 2004: A review of the reformed youth justice system*, London: Audit Commission.

Criminal Justice and Immigration Act 2008; www.opsi.gov.uk/acts/acts2008/ukpga_20080004_en_1

DCSF (Department for Children, Schools and Families) (2007) *The Children's Plan: Building brighter futures*, London: DCSF.

DCSF and DIUS (Department for Innovations, Universities and Skills) (2008) *Raising expectations: Enabling the system to deliver*, London: DCSF.

DfES (Department for Education and Skills) (2007) *Education for young people supervised by the youth justice system: A consultation*, London: DfES.

Hayward, G., Stephenson, M. and Blyth, M. (2004) 'Exploring educational opportunities for young people who offend', in R. Burnett and C. Roberts (eds) *What works in probation and youth justice: Developing evidence based practice*, Cullompton: Willan.

HM Government (2008) *Youth Crime Action Plan 2008*, London: COI.

HMIP (Her Majesty's Inspectorate of Prisons) and YJB (Youth Justice Board) (2005) *Juveniles in custody 2003-2004: An analysis of children's experiences of prison*, London: HMIP/YJB.

HM Inspectorate of Probation (2006) *Joint Inspection of YOTs 2005/6*, London: Home Office.

Offender Management Act (2007) Explanatory notes 144/5.

One Nottingham (2008) *Local area agreement*, www.onenottingham.com.

Solomon, E. and Garside, R. (2008) *Ten years of Labour's youth justice reforms: An independent audit*, London: Centre for Crime and Justice Studies.

Stephenson, M. (2007) *Young people and offending. Education, youth justice and social inclusion*, Cullompton: Willan.

YJB (Youth Justice Board) (2002) *Assessment of the Detention and Training Order and its impact across the secure estate*, London: YJB.

YJB (2004) *Summary of ISSP: the initial report*, London: YJB.

YJB (2005a) *Strategy for the Secure Estate for Children and Young People*, London: YJB.

YJB (2005b) *A summary of risk and protective factors associated with youth crime and effective interventions to prevent it*, London: YJB.

YJB (2005c) 'A review of the National Specification for Learning and Skills for young people by ECOTEC' (unpublished), London: YJB.

YJB (2007) *Corporate and business plan 2006/7-2008/09*, London: YJB.

YJB (2008a) *Key elements of effective practice* (updated), London: YJB.

YJB (2008b) *Youth justice annual workload data, 2006/7*, London: YJB.

7

Young people and parole: risk aware or risk averse?

Hazel Kemshall

Introduction and context

The United Kingdom currently has one of the highest juvenile prison populations in Western Europe (Goldson, 2005). This is against a backdrop of falling crime rates but heightened public, media and political perceptions to the contrary (Pitts, 2000, 2003; Tonry, 2004). The Commissioner for Human Rights noted that 'juvenile trouble-makers' in the UK were 'too rapidly drawn into the criminal justice system and young offenders are too readily placed in detention' (UN Committee on the Rights of the Child, 1995; Council of Europe Office of the Commissioner for Human Rights, 2005: 27). As Goldson (1999; see Goldson and Coles in this volume) has pointed out, the decade following the murder of Jamie Bulger in the UK saw a 'punitive populist' response to youth crime, with a doubling of custodial sentences since 1992, in a decade that has seen youth crime decrease by 16% (Nacro, 2003).

Perceived scandals and crises in parole and the community management of offenders (including young offenders) have also resulted in an increased tightening of the system. Recent years have seen an unprecedented amount of official guidance given to criminal justice agencies on the assessment and management of high-risk offenders. Nash (2006) identifies 12 probation circulars on this issue in 2005, and 2006 saw six circulars and *The risk of harm guidance and training resource* (version 3) (Kemshall et al, 2008), with a significant upturn following the publication of the serious further offence reports on Hanson and White, and Anthony Rice (HMI Probation, 2006a, 2006b). These reports highlighted both practice and process deficiencies in the assessment and management of high-risk offenders, and served to sharpen the debate about public protection. Such scandals and crises result in overt regulation within which the regulation and accountability of decision making becomes politicised. This is evidenced by the comments of the then incoming Home Secretary John Reid who stated:

> Reasonable people would view the decision to release someone that appears to emphasize the rights of a convicted murderer over the rights of his potential victims as tragically and disastrously mistaken. (Home Secretary, 2006, p 1)

The Home Secretary continued this theme, stating: 'The public has the right to expect that everything possible will be done to minimise the risk from serious violent and dangerous offenders' (Home Secretary, 2006, p 1), an expectation that was quickly translated into a 'dramatic overhaul of public protection arrangements' and a rebalancing of justice between offenders and victims (Home Office, 2006; Home Secretary, 2006). In respect of parole, the Home Secretary announced proposals to enhance the public protection focus of the Parole Board, including: unanimous verdicts on serious offenders; the use of 'public protection advocates' to represent victims' and society's views; and review of whether parole supervision and the whole process were sufficiently 'joined up' (Home Secretary, 2006, pp 1-5).

Interestingly, the Parole Board responded to this challenge by reiterating its existing expertise around victim experience and its members' familiarity with victim views (Parole Board, 2006a), by emphasising that current panel processes lead to unanimous views and highlighting the research that identified good practice (Hood and Shute, 2000). Alongside this, the Parole Board (2004) *Corporate plan 2004-07* targeted risk assessment as a key strategic aim, reiterated in the *Annual business plan* 2006-07 (Parole Board, 2006b):

> **To make risk assessments which are timely, rigorous, fair and consistent and which protect the public while contributing to the rehabilitation of prisoners so that effective decisions about prisoners can be made as to who may safely be released into the community and who must remain in or be returned to custody. (Parole Board, 2006b, para 2.2)**

Paralleling these initiatives, parole decisions for release fell in the first quarter after the publication of the Hanson and White report (HMI Probation, 2006a), indicating a degree of risk aversion and defensiveness. There was a drop in released lifers to one in nine of those considered, which represented a drop of 50% on the previous year (BBC news, 2006; see also Parole Board, 2006c, 2006d).

Sir Duncan Nichol, the former chair of the Parole Board, stated that there had been 'greater caution' in parole decisions following the HMI Probation reports. He stated that the Board 'will be absolutely sure before release' (BBC news, 2006).

Young people and parole

Young offenders are dealt with under this largely adult-focused system, although the High Court, in upholding a judicial review on a boy (K, aged 14), ruled that the Parole Board must be 'especially scrupulous' in ensuring fairness in its dealings with young offenders (see *R [K] v Parole Board [2006]*), and that its adult practice may require adaptation for youth cases (Stone, 2008). In January 2008 the management board of the Parole Board agreed that all extended sentence for public protection (EPP) parole applicants under 18 years old should automatically be referred to an oral hearing (Stone, 2008).[1] The Howard League has also stated that the 'law requires more exacting standards of fairness on the part of authorities dealing with children than would normally be necessary or appropriate in the case of an adult'. Its report argues for 'special mechanisms for a child going through the parole process' (Howard League, 2008, p 1). These concerns have also focused attention on the decision making of the Parole Board in respect of young offenders.

Improving decision making

A key response to 'faulty' decision making is to formalise it, usually through the use of risk-assessment tools. ASSET is the key tool for young offenders, although the tool has been criticised for: its lack of integrity in use (Baker et al, 2003; Baker, 2007); lack of consistency and poor rates of completion (Howard League, 2008, p 8); and a lack of commitment to the use of ASSET by workers (Kemshall, 2007a). Is the current risk of harm section fit for purpose and does it enable the Parole Board to make effective decisions about the future risk of harm posed by the young person?

The ASSET risk of harm section considers the following to be key factors in the identification of cases of concern:

- evidence of any harm-related behaviour by the young person, including behaviour under preparation, particular victim characteristics, offender factors and the results of any harmful behaviour (including any unintentional results);
- pattern, frequency and severity of harmful behaviour;
- current static and dynamic risk indicators; and
- assessment of future harmful behaviour (ASSET, Risk of Serious Harm: Full Assessment).

This information will need to be supplemented by a full 'pen picture' of the young person, including any information about trauma, abuse and victimisation, and is addressed by the Youth Justice Board (YJB) *Multi-agency public protection arrangements (MAPPA): Guidance for YOTs* (YJB, 2006a, p 8, p 10; see also YJB, 2005, 2006b). However, high-risk young offenders may of course present with a limited 'track record' of offending and little or no custodial experience, and those young offenders who commit a 'grave crime'[2] early in their careers present particular assessment issues (Boswell, 1997, 2007), particularly for parole boards. Young offenders who commit a serious or 'grave crime' as a first offence do not necessarily go on to commit further offences

---

[1] Note that the amendments contained within the Criminal Justice and Immigration Act have resulted in EPPs being released after serving one half of their custodial term without direction from the Parole Board.

of this type (Bailey, 1996; Boswell, 1997, 2007). This distinguishes them from those young offenders who progress through other types of violent crime and for whom past violent behaviour continues to be the best predictor of future violent behaviour (Hamilton, et al, 2002; Falshaw, 2005; Losel and Bender, 2006). Early identification of potentially violent offenders has proved problematic, as has the concept of 'career' for such offenders. However, early aggressiveness, and its continuation throughout childhood, appears to be an indicator of future violent offending (Farrington and West, 1993; Farrington, 1995, 1998). It is also important to note that young offenders who commit serious violent offences are not necessarily specialist and do commit other offences (Farrington, 1995, 1998).

In addition, to what extent is the information presented to the Parole Board fit for purpose and does the overall parole dossier enable an informed, robust, rigorous and fair risk assessment? Difficulties have been noted with the quality of parole reports (HMI Probation, 2006a; Kemshall, 2007b), including those for young offenders (Howard League, 2008), resulting in guidance from the YJB (2007). The knowledge base and expertise of practitioners, particularly at oral hearings, has also been questioned (Howard League, 2008), and expertise in the more specific tools for youth violence or for young offenders who sexually abuse is rare both within the secure estate and within Youth Offending Teams (YOTs) (see the training content in Kemshall et al, 2008).

The YJB guidance (2007) states that YOTs must provide the Parole Board with a report covering the following:

- an analysis of the index offence;
- details of the pattern of offending and any background information relating to risk, including a description and interpretation of all episodes causing or risking serious harm;
- information on behaviour and progress in custody, including any risk-reduction work undertaken and an assessment of the likely effectiveness;
- any medical, psychiatric and psychological considerations;
- risk assessment and management plan (including a vulnerability assessment and a consideration of factors that might influence risk and protective factors); and
- conclusions and recommendations (including a recommendation as to release and any additional licence conditions) (YJB, 2007, p 10).

---

[2] For example, those crimes committed by an offender aged between 10 and 17, which, if committed by an adult, would be punishable by 14 years or more, section 53 of the 1933 Children and Young Persons Act and section 91 of the 2000 Powers of Criminal Courts (Sentencing) Act, section 90 of the 2000 Powers of Criminal Courts (Sentencing) Act, section 61 of the 2000 Criminal Justice and Courts Act.

However highly regulated and prescriptive, rules for decision making do not necessarily improve decisions (see Kemshall, 2007b on parole decisions) and quality is not necessarily delivered by recourse to proceduralisation. Quality tends to concern itself with improving judgement; knowledge and reasoning on risk regulation tends to concern itself with the imposition and enforcement of prescriptive rules. The latter tends to require tight procedures, clear definitions of risk and high degrees of certainty. This is not always possible in this area. For example, Scott some 30 years ago argued that 'the legal category, even murder, arson and rape, is not very useful in determining dangerousness' (Scott, 1977, p 129), and that rather complex judgements based on the interaction of offender, circumstances and victim, combined with in-depth knowledge of behaviour, attitudes and motivation, is required (Kemshall et al, 2008). While there are a number of significant issues in 'knowing' high-risk or dangerous offenders, policy legislation and practice are all conducted as if we can know them. As Nash points out, 'the "pool" of potentially dangerous offenders is enormous' (Nash, 2006, p 21), comprising anyone who has the capacity to act harmfully. The trick is to discern with a reasonable degree of accuracy and consistency who might. In Home Office parlance this is the 'critical few' (Home Office, 2004). Knowing the 'critical few' requires high levels of expertise. As Nash succinctly puts it:

> Effective assessment of risk is dependent not only upon gathering as much information as possible, but also on making the best use of it. It also requires a constant updating of the information and analysis, especially in the case of young offenders who may be changing and developing at a rapid rate. (Nash, 2007, p 91)

What expertise is required?

Relevant expertise by both Parole Board members and practitioners has been advocated (Howard League, 2008), although this remains somewhat embryonic and aspirational. It is important to acknowledge the test that the Parole Board will apply – in essence, whether it is safe to release based on the level of assessed risk to the public (see, for example, *Secretary of State's directions to the Parole Board* [Home Office, 2006]). However, the YJB guidance points out that the test will be applied differently depending on whether the young person has received a determinate or indeterminate sentence (YJB, 2007). For indeterminate cases, the Board will assess whether 'the young person's "risk to life and limb" (of potential victims) is more than minimal' (YJB, 2007, p 11). For determinate sentences, the Board will consider whether the young person poses a risk of reoffending during the period they would otherwise have been in custody, and:

> ... whether such a risk is acceptable. This must be balanced against the benefit, both to the public and the young person, of early release under supervision, which might help rehabilitation. The Parole Board must take into account that safeguarding the public may often outweigh the benefits of early release. The risk of further violent

or sexual offending is regarded as more serious than a risk of other offending. (YJB, 2007, p 1)

The threshold of risk for indeterminate sentences is necessarily high. For determinate sentences, parole report writers are required to balance the risk of reoffending against the potential gains of supervision and the longer-term possibility of reducing risk through a parole-based intervention. Practitioners are also required to assess the imminence as well as the likelihood of the risk of reoffending harmfully, and to state how risks can be effectively managed within the community and whether the young person will comply (YJB, 2007, p 12).

Such analysis and judgement require high levels of expertise and an extensive knowledge base such as:

- knowledge of risk factors and the patterns and circumstances of sexual and violent offending pertinent to young offenders;
- knowledge of the development and maturation process of young people; the Court of Appeal ruling in the case of Lang (R v Lang and 12 others (2005) 2 All ER 410) stated that children may 'change and develop ... within a shorter time than adults' and that 'their level of maturity may be highly pertinent when assessing what their future conduct may be and whether it may give rise to significant risk of serious harm' (see also Howard League, 2008);
- knowledge of thinking patterns and cognitive skills of the young person;
- familiarity with key risk-assessment tools for high-risk youth, for example, the structured assessment of violence risk in youth (SAVRY) (Borum et al, 2006), and specific risk-assessment tools for youth who sexually abuse;
- knowledge of childcare legislation, including the complex needs of children 'in need';
- expertise and access to relevant services and resources required to effectively resettle and risk manage young offenders back into the community;
- knowledge of how young people make decisions on risk, and the processes associated with a transition away from risky behaviours and crime (Wikstrom, 2002, 2004a, 2004b); and
- knowledge of the factors that contribute to desistance from crime, the role of protective factors and mechanisms of resilience to crime pathways (Maruna, 2001; Bottoms et al, 2004; Kemshall et al, 2006).

These requirements set a high standard for the knowledge base and professional practice of YOT workers, which is only partially addressed by the YJB's attention to effective practice through guidance and training packs. The challenge for the Parole Board is perhaps more demanding. Given the rise in oral hearings (including those for juveniles and young offenders) it may not be possible to use only Board members with knowledge and expertise of youth offending on panels, as this will inevitably create delays (Stone, 2008). In addition, members are recruited as lay people, and it is reasonable to presume that this will not necessarily offer high levels of expertise. In essence, Board members are highly dependent on the quality of information gathering and analysis offered by those who compile the parole dossier and provide reports. Such reports are key and their quality is crucial (see YJB, 2007).

The Parole Board has also taken steps to quality assure its decision making, not least because of external criticism (HMI Probation, 2006a, 2006b; Home Secretary, 2006), the role of oral hearings and judicial review (Padfield, 2007), and the role of its own internal review committee, which provides peer scrutiny of release decisions where the offender has gone on to commit a sexual or violent offence (Stone, 2008). This has provided a greater focus on the 'defensibility' of such decisions.

Defensive or defensible practice?

Politicians and the public may assume that the Parole Board is about risk avoidance and aversion. However, the Board may describe its task as calculated risk taking, and indeed it contends that it does this reasonably well (Hood and Shute, 2000; Nichol, 2007; Shute, 2007). However, the political and policy climate of crime risk management may be described as predominantly risk averse (Kemshall, 2003), including the management and regulation of young people and young offenders (Case, 2007; Kemshall, 2008a). Where risk aversion predominates, we tend to see a reduction in the autonomy of frontline decision makers (and in this case Parole Board members). This can take place in at least three ways: executive control (that is, via Home Secretary instructions and guidance, and changes in legislation; for example, the 2007 Criminal Justice and Immigration Act); judicial control via challenges and reviews; and internally through internal guidance, standards, training and targets. The latter are often developed in response to the pressure exerted by executive control. This has resulted in a recent High Court finding, in the case of Brooke, that the workings of the Parole Board 'do not sufficiently demonstrate its objective independence' (Epstein, 2008, p 29). While this does not extend to individual cases or the decisions of individual Parole Board members, the court found that:

> ...the relationship of sponsorship is such as to create what objectively appears to be a lack of independence, and to cause the sponsoring department sometimes to treat the Board as part of its establishment. That has led to documented examples of the use of the powers of the department which have not been consistent with the need to maintain the Board's objective independence; those have been powers of funding, of appointment and to give directions. The continuing practice of regular confidential meetings between the Board and one party to its decisions (the Secretary of State for Justice), and the appearance given by the integration of the Board with the Justice Department for housing and email might not, alone, be inconsistent with the necessary demonstration of objective independence, but taken together with the other incidents of sponsorship they are. (Epstein, 2008, p 29)

As a result, the Parole Board has moved from being an executive body to being a court, with a strong likelihood of becoming a public protection court in the future (Parole Board, 2008). In a climate of risk aversion, practice can become defensive, resulting in blame shifting, blame avoiding, risk shifting and a general mentality of 'back covering' (Kemshall, 2008b). While it is difficult to identify any particular trend in respect of young people (Board statistics do not record decisions on young offenders separately), it is possible to identify some important broader trends:

- A Prisoner serving Imprisonment for Public Protection (IPP) beyond tariff term because of the lack of prison programmes and therefore the prisoner's inability to demonstrate a reduction in their risk. The Board cannot recommend release unless it is 'safe to do so' – attendance and compliance with a programme are often taken as evidence of reduced risk and increased safety.
- The volume of IPPs presented to the Parole Board for release decisions and the delays that have ensued (Parole Board, 2008). Legislative changes have taken place in the 2008 Criminal Justice Act (CJA) to remove the imposition of short minimum-term IPPs but it is unclear what impact this will have.
- The volume of oral hearings and judicial reviews that the Board is dealing with (Parole Board, 2008; Stone, 2008). The Parole Board estimates that the number of oral hearings may rise by 400% in the next six years, with judicial reviews reaching new record levels (Parole Board, 2008).
- The rising number of recalls, for example, on life licences, increasing from 34 in 1999 to 111 in 2005 (Offender Management Caseload Statistics 2005, England and Wales, Home Office, cited in Prison Reform Trust, 2007, p 9; see also Harding, 2006).

These trends are in large part a product of a penal policy driven by 'public protection' concerns and risk aversion on behalf of politicians and senior policy makers (Kemshall, 2008a, 2008b). They form the broader context within which the Parole Board is operating and, combined with the potential problems associated with independence noted above, they may have a significant impact on the defensible practice of the Board.

Conclusion: decision making in a complex risk system – drifting towards defensive practice?

Parole decisions are made within a particular context and errors in decision making are often attributable to other factors beyond the immediate actions of an individual (or individual panel) (see: Kemshall [2007b] for a full discussion on parole; and Leape [1994] and Reason [2000] for analysis of decision-making errors in complex risk systems). The initial error is often attributed to one key decision maker; however, the error is often 'best seen as the product of interaction between the individual and environment and … is likely to be the culmination of a series of events and combinations of circumstance which eventually come together' (Lloyd-Bostock and Hutter, 2008, p 78).

Research into complex systems of risk management from a number of fields – nuclear risk management, the oil industry, health (see, for example, Donaldson, 2000), social care and criminal justice (Kemshall, 2008b) – indicates a number of threats to effective decision making on risk. In brief, these are: fragmentation of risk-management systems; systemic failures; corrective actions that are externally imposed without adequate knowledge; unintended consequences of corrective actions/policies; and the creation of a risk-averse culture (Hutter, 2008; Kurunmaki and Miller, 2008; Lloyd-Bostock and Hutter, 2008).

Fragmentation of risk-management systems can be common, resulting in risk assessment and management spread over a number of different agencies producing a fragmented responsibility and accountability for risk. The most significant flaws tend to be the failure to exchange critical information, the failure to communicate changes in risk status, divisions between those who assess risk and those who decide (for example, to release), and perhaps even those who subsequently manage that risk. This can result in a mismatch of assessment and management, and a lack of accountability for decisions made. These issues were present to varying degrees in the serious further offence reviews of Hanson and White, and Anthony Rice (HMI Probation, 2006a, 2006b).

Such complex systems are also prone to systemic faults, for example, the failure of key procedures (for example, providing quality parole reports, informing prisoners of the correct procedures). This can result in a lack of consistency in decision making, a lack of equity and a lack of integrity. Corrective actions are often externally imposed (for example, by the executive onto the Board) in order to deal with perceived failures. These actions usually arise retrospectively, formulated with the 'benefit of hindsight', and often in the shadow of a crisis, failure or scandal. In this climate, corrective actions are often not negotiated with key players and implementers, are overstated and are sometimes disembodied from the context of practice in which they must be implemented. They often fail to recognise that many faults are systemic, and do not deal with systems and processes but over-focus on correcting presumed practitioner failings (Kemshall, 2007b). Such actions are usually accompanied by blame and censure, although the use of blame as a strategy for ensuring compliance with corrective actions has been increasingly challenged (see Donaldson, 2000; Lloyd-Bostock and Hutter, 2008).

Corrective actions can also have unintended consequences, for example, resulting in more decisions against parole (there was a drop of 50% on the previous year following the HMI Probation [2006a, 2006b] reports; see also BBC news, 2006; Parole Board, 2006c, 2006d, 2008) and a rise in the number of judicial review challenges that due process has not been followed. There may be other unintended perverse consequences, such as prison overcrowding or an increase in recalls for 'technical' rather than serious reoffending (HMI Probation, 2005; Harding, 2006; Prison Reform Trust, 2007; Howard League, 2008).

Corrective actions can also create a risk-averse culture (and are often the product of a politically risk-averse culture). Agencies and workers/practitioners/board members may naturally fear blame and censure, with the potential result that 'risky' decisions are avoided. Over time there is potential for the balance to move from calculated risk taking to risk aversion, from defensibility to defensiveness. Interestingly, judicial review, instigated by prisoners questioning the fairness and due process of decisions, may prove to be a realistic barrier to the corrective actions and 'steers' of the executive. In addition, there is the growing internal guidance, standard setting and quality assurance of the Parole Board itself, focusing on fairness and child-centred practice, as well as safety. This has been given added impetus by outside bodies such as the Howard League and the Prison Reform Trust seeking to rebalance the system. Time will tell how successful these initiatives are in preventing a drift towards defensive and increasingly punitive practice that has little regard to the specific needs of young people.

References

Bailey, S. (1996) 'Adolescents who murder', *Journal of Adolescence*, vol 19, no 1, pp 19-39.

Baker, K. (2007) 'Risk in practice: systems and practitioner judgement', in M. Blyth, E. Solomon and K. Baker (eds) *Young people and 'risk'*, The Policy Press: Bristol.

Baker, K., Jones, S., Roberts, C. and Merrington, S. (2003) *The evaluation of validity and reliability of the Youth Justice Board's assessment for young offenders: Findings from the first two years of the use of ASSET*, London: YJB, www.youth-justice-board.gov.uk/Publications

BBC news (2006) news.bbc.co.uk/1/hi/uk/6119576.stm, reported 6 November.

Borum, R., Bartel, P. and Forth, A. (2006) *Manual for the structured assessment of violence risk in youth* (version 1), Tampa, FL: University of South Florida.

Boswell, G. (1997) 'The backgrounds of violent young offenders: the present picture', in V. Varma (ed) *Violence in children and adolescents*, London: Jessica Kingsley, pp 22-36.

Boswell, G. (2007) 'Young people and violence: balancing public protection with meeting needs', in M. Blyth, E. Solomon and K. Baker (eds) *Young people and 'risk'*, Bristol: The Policy Press, pp 39-52.

Bottoms, A., Shapland, J., Costello, A., Holmes, D. and Muir, G. (2004) 'Towards desistance: theoretical underpinnings for an empirical study', *Howard Journal of Criminal Justice*, vol 43, no 3, pp 368-89.

Case, S. (2007) 'Questioning the "evidence" of risk that underpins evidence-led youth justice interventions', *Youth Justice*, vol 7, no 2, pp 91-105.

Council of Europe Office of the Commissioner for Human Rights (2005) *Report by Mr Alvaro Gil-Robles, Commissioner for Human Rights, on his visit to the United Kingdom, 4-12 November 2004*, Strasbourg: Council of Europe.

Criminal Justice and Immigration Act (2008) www.opsi.gov.uk/acts/acts2008/ukpga_ 20080004_en_1

Donaldson, Sir L. (2000) *An organisation with a memory: Learning from adverse events in the NHS.* A report by the Chief Medical Officer, London: Department of Health.

Epstein, R. (2008) 'The Parole Board found "not sufficiently independent"', *Justice of the Peace*, vol 172, 19 January, pp 28-9.

Falshaw, L. (2005) 'The link between a history of maltreatment and subsequent offending behaviour', *Probation Journal*, vol 52, no 4, pp 423-34.

Farrington, D.P. (1995) 'The development of offending and antisocial behaviour from childhood: key findings from the Cambridge Study in delinquent development', *Journal of Child Psychology and Psychiatry*, vol 36, pp 929-64.

Farrington, D.P. (1998) 'Predictors, causes, and correlates of male youth violence', in M. Tonry and M.H. Moore (eds) *Youth violence*, Chicago, IL: University of Chicago Press, pp 421-72.

Farrington, D.P. and West, D. (1993) 'Criminal, penal and life histories of chronic offenders: risk and protective factors and early identification', *Criminal Behaviour and Mental Health*, vol 3, pp 492-523.

Goldson, B. (1999) 'Youth (in)justice: contemporary developments in policy and practice', in B. Goldson (ed) *Youth justice: Contemporary policy and practice*, Aldershot: Ashgate.

Goldson, G. (2005) 'Taking liberties: policy and the punitive turn', in H. Hendrick (ed) *Children and social policy: An essential reader*, Bristol: The Policy Press, pp 255-68.

Hamilton, C.E., Falshaw, L. and Browne, K. (2002) 'The link between recurrent maltreatment and offending behaviour', *International Journal of Offender Therapy*, vol 46, no 1, pp 75-94.

Harding, J. (2006) 'Some reflections on risk assessment, parole and recall', *Probation Journal*, vol 53, no 4, pp 389-96.

HMI (Her Majesty's Inspectorate of) Probation (2005) *Recalled prisoners: A short review of recalled adult male determinate-sentenced prisoners*, London: HMI Probation.

HMI Probation (2006a) *An independent review of a serious further offence case: Damien Hanson and Elliot White*, London: HMI Probation.

HMI Probation (2006b) *An independent review of a serious further offence case: Anthony Rice*, London: HMI Probation.

Home Office (2004) *MAPPA guidance: Protection through partnership* (version 1.2), London: Home Office.

Home Office (2006) *Secretary of State's directions to the Parole Board*, London: Parole Board, www.paroleboard.gov.uk (accessed February 2008).

Home Secretary (2006) *Annual speech to the Parole Board*, May 2006, London: Home Office, www.press.homeoffice.gov.uk

Hood, R. and Shute, S. (2000) *The parole system at work: A study of risk based decision making*, Home Office Research Study 202, London: Research, Development and Statistics Directorate, Home Office.

Howard League (2008) *Parole 4 kids: A review of the parole process for children in England and Wales*, London: The Howard League for Penal Reform.

Hutter, B. (2008) 'Risk regulation and health care', *Health, Risk and Society*, vol 10, no 1, pp 1-8.

Kemshall, H. (2003) *Understanding risk in criminal justice*, Milton Keynes: Open University and McGraw-Hill.

Kemshall, H. (2007a) 'Risk assessment and risk management: the right approach?', in M. Blyth, E. Solomon and K. Baker (eds) *Young people and 'risk'*, Bristol: The Policy Press, pp 7-23.

Kemshall, H. (2007b) 'MAPPA, parole and the management of high risk offenders in the community', in N. Padfield (ed) *Who gets out? Parole and criminal justice*, Cullumpton: Willan, pp 202-14.

Kemshall, H. (2008a) 'Risks, rights and justice: understanding and responding to youth risk', *Youth Justice*, vol 8, no 1, pp 21-38.

Kemshall, H. (2008b) *Understanding the community management of high risk offenders*, Milton Keynes: Open University and McGraw-Hill.

Kemshall, H., Mackenzie, G., Miller, J. and Wilkinson, B. (2008) *The risk of harm guidance and training resource* (version 3), CD ROM, Leicester: NOMS and De Montfort University.

Kemshall, H., Marsland, L., Boeck, T. and Dunkerton, L. (2006) 'Young people, pathways and crime: beyond risk factors', *Australian and New Zealand Journal of Criminology*, vol 39, no 3, pp 354-70.

Kurunmaki, L. and Miller, P. (2008) 'Counting the costs: the risks of regulating and accounting for health care provision', *Health, Risk and Society*, vol 10, no 1, pp 9-22.

Leape, L.L. (1994) 'Error in medicine', *Journal of the American Medical Association*, vol 272, pp 1851-7.

Lloyd-Bostock, S. and Hutter, B. (2008) 'Reforming regulation of the medical profession: the risks of risk-based approaches', *Health, Risk and Society*, vol 10, no 1, pp 69-84.

Losel, F. and Bender, D. (2006) 'Risk factors for serious violent antisocial behaviour in children and youth', in A. Hagell and R. Jeyarajah-Dent (eds) *Children who commit acts of serious interpersonal violence: Messages for best practice*, London: Jessica Kingsley.

Maruna, S. (2001) *Making good: How ex-convicts reform and rebuild their lives*, Washington, DC: American Psychological Association.

Nacro (2003) *A failure of youth justice: Reducing child imprisonment*, London: Nacro.

Nash, M. (2006) *Public protection and the criminal justice process*, Oxford: Oxford University Press.

Nash, M. (2007) 'Working with young people in a culture of public protection', in: M. Blyth, E. Solomon and K. Baker (eds) *Young people and 'risk'*, Bristol: The Policy Press, pp 85-96.

Nichol, D. (2007) 'Who should we keep locked up?' in N. Padfield (ed) *Who to release? Parole, fairness and criminal justice*, Cullumpton: Willan, pp 17-20.

Padfield, N. (ed) (2007) *Who to release? Parole, fairness and criminal justice*, Cullumpton: Willan.

Parole Board (2004) *Corporate plan 2004-2007*, London: Parole Board, www.paroleboard.gov.uk

Parole Board (2006a) *Parole Board response to Home Secretary's proposals for reform*, London: Parole Board, www.paroleboard.gov.uk.

Parole Board (2006b) *Annual business plan*, London: Parole Board, www.paroleboard.gov.uk

Parole Board (2006c) *Annual report 2005-06*, London: Parole Board, www.paroleboard.gov.uk

Parole Board (2006d) *Statistics 2005-06*, www.paroleboard.gov.uk

Parole Board, (2008) *Annual report and accounts 2007/8*, London: Parole Board.

Pitts, J. (2000) 'The new youth justice and the politics of electoral anxiety', in B. Goldson (ed) *The new youth justice*, Lyme Regis: Russell House Publishing.

Pitts, J. (2003) *The new politics of youth crime: Discipline or solidarity* (2nd edn), London: Russell House Publishing.

Prison Reform Trust (2007) *Indefinitely maybe? How the determinate sentence for public protection is unjust and unsustainable: A Prison Reform Trust briefing*, London: Prison Reform Trust, 31 July, wwwprisonreformtrust.org.uk

R [K] v Parole Board (2006) EWHC 2413 [Admin]

Reason, J. (2000) 'Human error: models and management', *British Medical Journal*, vol 320, pp 768-70.

Scott, P. (1977) 'Assessing dangerousness in criminals', *British Journal of Psychiatry*, vol 131, pp 127-42.

Shute, S. (2007) 'Parole and risk assessment', in N. Padfield (ed) *Who to release? Parole, fairness and criminal justice*, Cullompton: Willan.

Stone, N. (2008) Response to paper by H. Kemshall at the Young people and custody seminar, sponsored by Rainer, London, 1 Birdcage Walk, 22 April.

Tonry, M. (2004) *Punishment and politics: Evidence and emulation in the making of English crime control policy*, Cullompton: Willan.

UN Committee on the Rights of the Child (1995) *Concluding observations of the Committee on the Rights of the Child: United Kingdom of Great Britain and Northern Ireland*, CRC/C/14, Add 34, 15 February.

Wikstrom, P.-O.H. (2002) *Adolescent crime in context (the Peterborough Youth Study)*, Report to the Home Office, Cambridge: Institute of Criminology, Cambridge.

Wikstrom, P.-O.H. (2004a) 'Crime as an alternative: towards a cross-level situational action theory of crime causation', in J. McCord (ed) *Beyond empiricism: Institutions and intentions in the study of crime*, New Brunswick, NJ: Transaction, pp 1-38.

Wikstrom, P.-O.H. (2004b) 'The origins of patterns in offending. Towards a developmental ecological action theory of crime involvement', in D.P. Farrington (ed) *Testing integrated developmental/life course theories of offending. Advances in criminological theory*, New Brunswick, NJ: Transaction.

YJB (Youth Justice Board) (2005) *Managing risk in the community*, Effective practice reader prepared for the Youth Justice Board by B. Wilkinson and K. Baker, London: YJB, www.youth-justice-board.gov.uk.

YJB (2006a) *Multi-agency public protection arrangements (MAPPA): Guidance for YOTs*, London: YJB, www.youth-justice-board.gov.uk

YJB (2006b) *Criminal Justice Act 2003: 'Dangerousness' and the new sentences for public protection – guidance for youth offending*, London: YJB, www.youth-justice-board.gov.uk

YJB (2007) *Release and recall guidance*, London: YJB, www.youth-justice-board.gov.uk

8

Ten years on: conclusions

Robert Newman and Maggie Blyth

The contributions in this volume raise important policy questions with respect to three overlapping areas outlined in the Introduction: the suitability of the current custodial system for children and young people; the scope for more effective resettlement opportunties; and an examination of where accountability should reside for children and young people sent to custody. It is to this latter point that we now turn in our conclusions.

The legacy of organic growth

Any analysis of custodial provision for children and young people is likely to be somewhat critical and bleak in outlook. The sentencing of a young person to custody is, by its very nature, an admission of failure by a system struggling to square the competing demands for punishment and rehabilitation. It is an imperfect system and the contributors here pull no punches in identifying its shortcomings. But, before looking at the contributions in a little more detail, it may be worth dwelling briefly on some of the features of custody prior to 1999, three years after *Misspent youth* (Audit Commission, 1996) criticised the system for its costliness and its inability to reduce reoffending. The incoming New Labour administration responded in 1997 with *No more excuses* (Home Office, 1997) in which it also acknowledged that custodial provision was unsatisfactory. Both of these publications were influential in setting the foundations for the reform of custodial provision implemented subsequently over the last decade and providing the context for some of the current debate outlined in the Youth Crime Action Plan (YCAP) (HM Government, 2008).

Many commentators, including those in this volume (see Chapters 1 and 3), highlight the steep rise in the use of custody after 1991, and *No more excuses* recognised that no system had been devised, much less implemented, to cope with the secure estate population explosion during the 1990s. The process of placement into custody was at that time a lottery, with little regard for the young person's needs and a rigid dispersal policy driven by a system of feeder courts with regular deliveries by the escort service. Young people were routinely transported with adults and accommodated in adult establishments. There were no agreed regime standards for children, despite increasing scrutiny from the United Nations Convention on the Rights of the Child (UNCRC), and 23-hours-a-day lock-up was not unusual. When the Youth Justice Board (YJB) was formed in 1998, the development of the previous government's flagship secure training centre (STC) programme was stalling following the commissioning of the first two centres, despite New Labour's commitment to continue it. Issues of cost and accountability related to custody were confused, making it impossible to determine the effectiveness of the system in the absence of any agreed standards.

Towards centralisation

A decade ago, *No more excuses* heralded a bold and unprecedented reform programme for youth justice. It proposed a new statutory aim for the youth justice system with duties on local agencies to join forces in tackling youth crime. As well as widening the range of community penalties available, it announced the Detention and Training Order (DTO) and made much of the need for joined-up post-custodial supervision. Its section on 'Effective custodial penalties and remands' provided the blueprint for what the YJB subsequently developed into its own strategy for the secure estate. The intention to develop custodial provision more systematically through standard setting, monitoring, purchasing and commissioning responsibilities was comprehensively set out in *No more excuses.*

Interestingly, although the report clearly recommended the need for a centrally driven administration, there was a clear focus on the home local authority retaining a degree of responsibility for the young person throughout custody. There was an expectation that the Youth Offending Team (YOT) would maintain oversight of the sentence plan, including the custodial element. It was also envisaged that local authorities would play a much greater role in placement than was eventually the case: 'The new arrangements will allow the Home Secretary to delegate the responsibility for placements to local youth offending teams, rather than having placements decided centrally' (Home Office, 1997, p 22). These arrangements for local placement decision making have never been implemented and the wider issue of local authority responsibility for young people in custody and after release has remained contentious, resurfacing in the YCAP (HM Government, 2008).

The system under pressure

Rod Morgan (Chapter 1) reflects on the evolution of the juvenile secure estate under the stewardship of the YJB, referring to the purchasing and commissioning role that the YJB took on in 2000 as a 'poisoned chalice'. He comments on the 'British addiction to the punishment of the young' as contributing to the increase in custodial numbers over two decades, and concludes that New Labour has done nothing to 'reverse the trend' inherited from the Conservatives.

In describing some of the challenges faced by the YJB in reforming the system, Morgan acknowledges the disappointingly weak impact of the purchaser-provider split in creating market conditions that have any real leverage to drive up standards. He also touches on some of the complex issues raised by the use of the private sector.

Morgan concludes that there may be a ray of hope in the new joint accountability arrangements for the YJB with the two ministers 'wrestling … over the carcass of youth justice and the work of the YJB', but remarks that the YCAP does not signal any change of policy direction in relation to custody.

With regard to the more punitive sentencing climate, there appear to be different responses in how young people are dealt with across the country, and inconsistent sentencing across geographical, gender and ethnicity boundaries is highlighted by Kerry Baker (Chapter 4) where she examines in more detail the complexities of the sentencing decision. This impacts not only on the numbers of young people in custody but also on the length of time they are incarcerated. Baker goes on to highlight the confusion over the purpose of sentencing, which falls between the principal aim of the youth justice system – prevention – and the four other purposes applied to the adult system under the 2003 Criminal Justice Act. If these labyrinthine considerations are 'unintelligible' to the judiciary, it is unlikely that they will inspire the confidence of the public. Baker is equally circumspect about whether the new Youth Rehabilitation Order ('YRO'), which has been hailed as streamlining community sentencing, will have the desired effect. She is concerned that the YRO, with its menu of interventions, may remove any sense of tariff or progression before custody is imposed.

The context of public attitudes and the expectations that drive 'penal populism' are all important in considering the sentencing decision and Baker urges more work to explore the role of the practitioner. There are no quick fixes and it is vital that we recognise the value of research in informing practice.

Cost and quality

Jim Rose (Chapter 2) attempts to 'get under the skin' of the custodial regime to look at the impact of the culture and ethos of an establishment on the staff and young people who interact behind 'the wire'. Rose traces the evolution of the three types of custody currently comprising the secure estate for children and young people: the young offender institutions (YOIs) with their roots in penal services; the secure children's homes (SCHs) serving a dual criminal justice and welfare role with roots in residential childcare; and the STCs, a hybrid, designed specifically to bridge the divide. In advocating the importance of a stong and supportive external management structure to develop the sort of 'containing environment' necessary to meet the needs of young people, Rose is critical of the Prison Service's failure to develop discrete management arrangements for its juvenile estate. He is also concerned about the impact of financial penalties and the drive for contractual compliance in the private sector on the prioritisation of welfare issues.

The assertion that staff are the most valuable resource in any residential environment is not new, but Rose goes further to explore the complex interactions between staff and young people that occur in the context of the 'daily routines of residential living'.

The importance of the minutiae of the group living experience and the way the staff dress and address the young people are all vital elements in determining the culture and ethos of any institution, as important as any formal programme delivery. Rose questions whether the development of an 'effective pro-social modelling approach' is achievable given current staff recruitment and training arrangements and the fact that staffing ratios in many establishments are still woefully inadequate.

For all its faults, the commissioning and purchasing system set up by the YJB in 1999 does provide us with a clearer picture of what custody actually costs. Rob Allen (Chapter 3) develops the theme further by exploring whether, in making local authorities responsible for bearing the costs of custody instead of central government, this would result in more investment from local agencies in intensive and sustained community-based programmes or targeted prevention. Despite a lack of conclusive evidence, Allen speculates about whether the current system could be incentivising 'cost shunting' in which local authorities fail to make expensive interventions in the knowledge that central government will pay if the young person offends and goes into custody. Allen's use of the 'justice reinvestment' model draws on research undertaken in the US that demonstrates the value of transferring costs in this way and incentivising more integrated preventive children's services. It is no secret that the idea of transferring the costs of custody to local authorities was hotly debated across government in the run-up to the publication of the YCAP (HM Government, 2008). The plan stopped short of proposing the piloting of custodial costs transfer in favour of beefing up local authority duties in relation to resettlement and committing to transferring the costs of court-ordered secure remands.

It is perhaps too simplistic to assume that transferring responsibility for the cost of custody alone will reduce its usage. The sentencing decision is complex and varied. Local authorities alone may not always be in as influential a position as one might expect in working with the judiciary. Nevertheless, current government policy does commit to making the costs of custody 'more visible': 'to help inform the debate on whether in the longer term, local authorities should be responsible for placement [sic] and funding of custodial placements' (HM Government, 2008, p 70). As Allen concludes, this isn't just an exercise in accountancy, but more about 'strengthening and integrating the preventive and rehabilitative response to this group'.

High stakes

Within the secure estate for children and young people there is a much smaller group of around 500 at any given time (YJB, 2008b) who have been convicted of very serious crimes. They are serving long sentences and their release involves the consideration of serious public protection factors. Hazel Kemshall (Chapter 7) explores the interplay of influences that affect parole decisions for young people. Kemshall concludes that the recent drop in the number of parole decisions directing release is evidence of increasing risk aversion. She acknowledges that, although important concessions have recently been made affecting parole decisions for young people under the age of 18, the system remains largely an adult-focused process. Risk assessment in relation to young people is often difficult (Blyth et al, 2007) and information sparse in assisting the Parole Board with necessary evidence to inform decision making. With a paucity of expertise in the assessment of violent and sexually abusing young people and the increasing drift towards highly regulated and prescriptive risk assessment, there is an argument for ensuring that the Parole Board applies approaches to decisions about release that are appropriate to the distinctive needs of young people and draws on specialist expertise.

Much of the debate about predicting risk is linked to assessment, but some of the key dilemmas relate specifically to the assessment of young people's risk of serious harm to others and, in particular, to themselves. Barry Goldson and Deborah Coles (Chapter 5) investigate the structural and institutional conditions that, they argue, lead to death, harm and damage to children in penal custody. With a wealth of experience in analysing post-death investigations and inquests, Goldson and Coles are categorically in favour of progressive reform that looks at alternative measures to custody. While Goldson and Coles acknowledge the high levels of activity by government bodies responsible for custody designed to make it safer to reduce the risk of injury and death, they pose a critical question: is the totality of these measures to improve the regime and custodial environment ever going to be adequate to address the systemic failings the evidence suggests are at the heart of most serious incidents? They conclude that there is a lack of evidence that the policies, practices and procedures adopted over the last decade have succeeded in eliminating the risk of injury and death of children in custody. An effective starting point, as far as they are concerned, is the instigation of an independent commission to investigate the deaths of children and young people in custody, which leads to clear recommendations for a review of youth custody.

The third way

Certainly, there are a number of coinciding factors that suggest that now is perhaps the time to review the DTO a decade into the youth justice reforms. Maggie Blyth and Robert Newman (Chapter 6) pick up the challenge in proposing a new hybrid sentence with education at its centre. They argue that the evidence base linking education and employment to offending, and disappointment over whether the DTO has fulfilled its promise on re-engagement, support the case for a different approach. They also question whether a sentencing structure based on an adult criminal justice model is necessarily the best approach to rehabilitating young people. Current developments within children's services and integrated youth support, with a heavy emphasis on early intervention, the development of the 14-19 agenda and the proposed new duties on local authorities in respect of offender learning, and the new purpose for sentencing and the changes to community sentencing embodied in the YRO provide a context for such a review.

Blyth and Newman outline the case for an Education Placement Order (EPO) to reduce the current custodial population by targeting those young people who do not present significant public protection risks and providing a resettlement opportunity for those who have spent time in custody. Using existing residential education providers, the proposal could be more cost-effective than some of our current custodial placements.

Conclusion

The youth justice reforms have undoubtedly delivered some improvements to youth custody over the last decade. It is recognised that young people in custody must have access to mainstream services, particularly health, substance misuse and education, with improved links to local safeguarding services (YJB, 2005). Although the aspiration to develop a completely discrete juvenile secure estate has not yet been realised, children under 15 are no longer placed in Prison Service accommodation and more children are now placed in discrete establishments for the under 18s as opposed to mixed campuses – 42% in 2004 to 58% in 2008 (YJB, 2008b). There have also been notable improvements in capital infrastructure and staff training (YJB, 2008c). There have undoubtedly been clear benefits in centralising the management of the secure estate for children and young people, albeit there is still a long way to go. However, one unintended consequence of this necessarily 'centralist' approach to custodial reform adopted since 1999 is that some local authorities may have found it easier to adopt an 'out of sight, out of mind' attitude to their young people in custody, making re-engagement with mainstream services post-release even more problematic. YOTs have sometimes struggled to broker access to mainstream education, health and housing with statutory agencies, and young people in the youth justice system have remained detached from essential provision.

Despite a performance framework designed to hold local agencies to account from the centre, young people in the youth justice system remain the most marginalised. It is to be hoped that the new joint accountability for youth justice at national level and the clear messages about local authority responsibilities set out in the YCAP will signal a new era for youth justice services. The increased local authority stake in custody and new duties in relation to resettlement and education at least provide the opportunity to incentivise the development of early intervention models and intensive community programmes that reduce our dependence on custody as a primary means of punishing young people and reducing youth crime.

References

Audit Commission (1996) *Misspent youth: Young people and crime*, London: Audit Commission.

Blyth, M., Solomon, E. and Baker, K. (2007) *Young people and risk*, Bristol: The Policy Press.

HM Government (2008) *Youth Crime Action Plan 2008*, London: COI.

The Home Office (1997) *No more excuses – A new approach to tackling youth crime*, London: Home Office.

YJB (Youth Justice Board) (2005) *Strategy for the Secure Estate for Children and Young People*, London: YJB.

YJB (2008a) Internal management information (unpublished).

YJB (2008b) *Workload data 2006/7*, London: YJB.

YJB (2008c) *Annual report and accounts 2007/8*, London: YJB.